CLASSICAL
CHRISTIAN DOCTRINE

INTRODUCING THE ESSENTIALS
of the ANCIENT FAITH

RONALD E. HEINE

Baker Academic
a division of Baker Publishing Group
Grand Rapids, Michigan

© 2013 by Ronald E. Heine

Published by Baker Academic
a division of Baker Publishing Group
P.O. Box 6287, Grand Rapids, MI 49516-6287
www.bakeracademic.com

Printed in the United States of America

Library of Congress Cataloging-in-Publication Data
Heine, Ronald E.
    Classical Christian doctrine : introducing the essentials of the ancient faith / Ronald E. Heine.
       p.   cm.
    Includes bibliographical references and index.
    ISBN 978-0-8010-4873-9 (pbk.)
      1. Theology—History—Early church, ca. 30–600. I. Title.
BT23.H45 2012
230′.11—dc23   2012034658

Unless noted otherwise, all Scripture translations are those of the author.

Scripture quotations marked NRSV are from the New Revised Standard Version of the Bible, copyright © 1989, by the Division of Christian Education of the National Council of the Churches of Christ in the United States of America. Used by permission. All rights reserved.

Scripture quotations marked KJV are from the King James Version of the Bible.

The internet addresses, email addresses, and phone numbers in this book are accurate at the time of publication. They are provided as a resource. Baker Publishing Group does not endorse them or vouch for their content or permanence.

13   14   15   16   17   18   19   7   6   5   4   3   2   1

In keeping with biblical principles of creation stewardship, Baker Publishing Group advocates the responsible use of our natural resources. As a member of the Green Press Initiative, our company uses recycled paper when possible. The text paper of this book is composed in part of post-consumer waste.

Contents

v

127117

Contents

Preface

The past several decades have seen an increased interest in returning to the ancient sources of the Christian faith. There has been an expanding interest in the academic field known as patristics, which is the study of the Christian writers of the first five centuries. There have been new commentary series that have drawn their explanations of the Scriptures from these early Christian authors. There has also been an increased interest in understanding what the early Christians believed. This book has been written to serve as a gateway into the beliefs and teachings of the early Christians. The doctrines treated in this book are those set forth in the Nicene Creed of the fourth century. I have used the creed to provide the topics discussed in the various chapters; however, the book is not a commentary on the creed. The inclusion of these topics in this important creed means that they were central topics in the early Christians' understanding of their faith. Some of the chapters focus on the topics before they reached their final formulation in the creed. Others reach some years beyond the creed as understandings expressed there were fleshed out in later debates. The chapter on Scripture (ch. 2) is an exception. There is no doctrine of Scripture in the statements of faith found in the Nicene Creed. A very definite concept of

Scripture, however, is presupposed and used in the creed. It is for this reason that I have included this chapter.

I have written this book to be used in undergraduate classes introducing students to the study of Christian doctrine. Short excerpts from original sources are placed in sidebars so the student can get an idea of how some of the early Christians reasoned and expressed themselves on these topics. The translations of these excerpts are my own, except where a translator or translation is indicated at the end of the excerpt. Each chapter concludes with questions for discussion and suggestions for further reading. These readings are primarily in translations from original sources. The book does not presuppose any special understanding or skills in theology. It is intended to be a primer. It might also be found useful for church groups interested in coming to grips with the roots of the Christian faith. It is offered in the service of him who said, "Take my yoke upon you, and learn from me. . . . For my yoke is easy, and my burden is light" (Matt. 11:29–30 NRSV).

Ronald E. Heine
October 2011

Abbreviations

General

ANF   *The Ante-Nicene Fathers.* Edited by Alexander Roberts and James Donaldson. 1885–87. 10 vols. Reprint, Grand Rapids: Eerdmans, 1951–53.

ch./chs. chapter/chapters

FOTC   The Fathers of the Church

KJV   King James Version

LCL   Loeb Classical Library

NHL   *The Nag Hammadi Library in English.* Edited by James M. Robinson. New York: Harper & Row, 1977.

NPNF *The Nicene and Post-Nicene Fathers.* Edited by Philip Schaff and Henry Wace. 1886–90. 1st and 2nd series. 28 vols. Reprint, Grand Rapids: Eerdmans, 1979–83.

NRSV   New Revised Standard Version

OTP   *The Old Testament Pseudepigrapha.* Edited by J. H. Charlesworth. 2 vols. New York: Doubleday, 1983, 1985.

PG   Patrologia graeca. Edited by J.-P. Migne. 162 vols. Paris, 1857–86.

v./vv.   verse/verses

Old Testament

Gen.	Genesis	Song	Song of Songs/Song of
Exod.	Exodus		Solomon
Lev.	Leviticus	Isa.	Isaiah
Deut.	Deuteronomy	Jer.	Jeremiah
Josh.	Joshua	Ezek.	Ezekiel
Judg.	Judges	Dan.	Daniel
Ps./Pss.	Psalm/Psalms		

New Testament

Matt.	Matthew	1–2 Thess.	1–2 Thessalonians
Rom.	Romans	1–2 Tim.	1–2 Timothy
1–2 Cor.	1–2 Corinthians	Philem.	Philemon
Gal.	Galatians	Heb.	Hebrews
Eph.	Ephesians	1–2 Pet.	1–2 Peter
Phil.	Philippians	Rev.	Revelation
Col.	Colossians		

Apocrypha

Bar.	Baruch	Wis.	Wisdom of Solomon
1–2 Macc.	1–2 Maccabees		

Old Testament Pseudepigrapha

2 Bar.	2 Baruch	1–2 En.	1–2 Enoch

Apostolic Fathers

Barn.	Epistle of Barnabas
1–2 Clem.	1–2 Clement
Did.	Didache
Herm. Mand.	Shepherd of Hermas, Mandate(s)
Herm. Sim.	Shepherd of Hermas, Similitude(s)
Herm. Vis.	Shepherd of Hermas, Vision(s)
Ign. Magn.	Ignatius, To the Magnesians
Ign. Smyrn.	Ignatius, To the Smyrnaeans
Ign. Trall.	Ignatius, To the Trallians
Pol. Phil.	Polycarp, To the Philippians

1

What Is Classical Christian Doctrine?

> Let that which you heard from the beginning
> remain in you.
>
> 1 John 2:24

Identifying the Major Personalities

Irenaeus: A Christian bishop in Lyons, France, in the last quarter of the second century; he was raised in the ancient Christian center of Smyrna (see Rev. 1:11 and 2:8) on the coast of Asia Minor (modern Turkey), where he knew Polycarp.

Polycarp: Bishop of Smyrna from the early to the mid-second century; may have known the apostle John; recipient of a letter from Ignatius; martyred at age eighty-six in the mid-second century.

Ignatius: Bishop of Antioch in Syria in the early second century; martyred in Rome, probably in the reign of Trajan (AD 98–117); authored seven letters as he was being taken to Rome to be executed.

"Doctrine" is a term that is often misunderstood. It is sometimes connected with particular views of the end of the world or with complicated views about who can receive salvation. Some Christians think that they hold no doctrines. They just believe in Jesus. But when one claims to believe in Jesus, that implies that one

1

believes certain things about Jesus, such as who he was or is and why believing in him is important. All Christians have always held doctrines about Jesus and other topics related to Jesus. It is important, therefore, to understand what these doctrines are and why they came to be. This book introduces the most basic doctrines of the Christian faith that have been held by a majority of Christians since the earliest centuries of the faith. I have called them classical Christian doctrines. But because the terms "classical" and "doctrine" can both be ambiguous, let's begin by offering definitions for what these terms will mean in this book.

A Definition of "Classical"

The word "classical" is somewhat elastic in its uses. We speak, for example, of classical music, classical architecture, and classical literature. I did my doctoral work in classical philology. In each of these uses the word "classical" has differing implications. "Classical music" may refer to a particular style of music, particular composers, a particular period of time in which the music was composed or, as is more usually the case, to a combination of some or all of these factors. "Classical architecture" usually refers to the architecture of the ancient Greeks and Romans stretching from perhaps the sixth century BC through the second century AD. "Classical literature" is usually the literature specific to a culture and may be delineated differently in the various cultures. In English-speaking culture "classical literature" certainly includes the works of authors like Chaucer and Shakespeare, but it is by no means limited to them. "Classical philology," on the other hand, in the Western academic world refers specifically to the study of the language and literature of the ancient Greeks and Romans. The classical period of the Greek language and literature is considered to begin with the Homeric epics called *The Iliad* and *The Odyssey* and to end with the writings of the great tragic and comic poets, the Athenian orators, and the philosophical

2

writings of Plato. When I was a university student, one of the professors in the classics department frequently referred to all Greek literature written after about the end of the fifth century BC as composed in the period of the decadence of the language. Unfortunately, he was on the examination committee for my dissertation, and I had written on a treatise of one of the church fathers who lived in the fourth century AD. He commented that I had done a good job on my dissertation, but that it should probably never have been written!

What might "classical Christian doctrine" mean? One of the implications of the adjective "classical" in all the examples considered in the preceding paragraph is that for something to be called classical, it must have endured. If Shakespeare's plays had not been read and performed after their first performance in the late sixteenth and early seventeenth centuries, they would not be considered classical. There is also an appeal factor in things that are labeled classical. They have a quality that appeals to and is recognized by a large number of people. Many people find them pleasing or, in the case of doctrines, correct.

What I mean by "classical Christian doctrine" in this book is those doctrines that were accepted as true by most Christians before the end of the first four centuries of the Christian era. The classical expression of these doctrines is found in summary format in the Nicene Creed.[1] This creed was drawn up by the first ecumenical council of the church, at Nicaea in AD 325, and was supplemented with a slight addition a few years later at the second ecumenical council, at Constantinople in AD 381. It has been, and continues to be, the most widely used expression of the Christian faith in the world. It is still today recited regularly in the worship services of Orthodox, Roman Catholic, and Protestant churches around the world.

This book is not a study of the Nicene Creed as such, but the creed provides the general doctrines that are considered in this book. Some of the chapters, however, are about doctrines that

1. The text of the Nicene Creed of AD 381 can be found in ch. 3.

3

were proposed as ways of understanding a particular topic but were ultimately rejected as inadequate by the larger group of Christians. Looking at some of the rejected viewpoints helps us better understand why Christians expressed a particular doctrine as they did, or why it was important to discuss a particular topic at all. A few of the doctrines discussed reached their final form of expression several years after the drawing up of the creed by the Council of Nicaea. Some were added at the Council of Constantinople in AD 381.

It was during the first four centuries of the Christian era that all the major doctrines of the church were set forth. These doctrines continue to be foundational for all later thought about what it means to be Christian. The importance of this period of time for Christian doctrine gives it the right to be considered the classical period of the Christian faith, and those doctrines defined in this period, classical Christian doctrines.

A Definition of "Doctrine"

The other term that needs to be defined is "doctrine." Christians often talk about doctrine. It is a regular part of the Christian vocabulary, so much so that it is sometimes thought to be a concept that belongs to church language alone. The English word "doctrine" is derived from the Latin word *doctrina*, which means "teaching" or "instruction." Every field of knowledge has a body of teachings that make up its doctrine. These teachings constitute the core of that discipline's self-understanding. Every person who practices that discipline shares these teachings and, in more or less completeness, follows them. If one is an analytical philosopher, for example, he or she will share with other analytical philosophers a particular view of reality, language, ways of speaking about reality, and ways of approaching and solving problems. The same could be said of nuclear physicists, biologists, ecologists, or any others who participate in a branch of learning or belief system. Each branch of learning has a body of doctrine. Those doctrines involve how people who share that discipline understand their discipline, and what they communicate about it, both in discussions with others who share the discipline and to those outside the discipline.

When we speak of "Christian doctrine," then, we are speaking of the Christian system of belief or the common core of Christian teaching that determines Christian self-understanding—that is, what it means to be a Christian. This represents what Christians believe in common and what they communicate to others. Christian doctrines have been defined by George Lindbeck as "communally authoritative teachings regarding beliefs and practices that are considered essential to the identity . . . of the group in question." "[T]hey indicate," he continues, "what constitutes faithful adherence to a community."[2] This last statement points to something very important about doctrines. They set boundaries.

Doctrines and Boundaries

Doctrines define acceptable and unacceptable views.[3] Christian doctrines are definitive by nature; that is, they define what it means to be Christian. The Christian writers of the classical period of Christian doctrine spoke often of heresies. A heretic was someone who believed and taught a doctrine that was not accepted by the larger body of Christian believers.

Irenaeus wrote a large treatise at the end of the second century AD that he called *An Examination and Overthrow of What Is Falsely Called Knowledge*. (This work is usually referred to simply as *Against Heresies*, which is the title that will be used throughout this book.)

The treatise is almost completely devoted to the heresy known as gnosticism. There were groups other than the gnostics who also held views that the larger body of Christians did not accept, but the issues raised by the gnostics were the subject of most

2. George A. Lindbeck, *The Nature of Doctrine* (London: SPCK, 1984), 74.
3. See Thomas C. Oden, *The Rebirth of Orthodoxy* (San Francisco: HarperSanFrancisco, 2003), 132–36.

discussions of heresy in the second century. Gnostics believed and taught a number of things about Jesus that the larger body of Christians did not accept as true. Some gnostics, for example, did not believe that Jesus had a real body of flesh. They thought he only appeared to have such a body. Without a body of flesh, he could not, of course, suffer and die. This view contradicted some core beliefs that the majority of Christians held about Jesus and what he had done for them.

Some gnostics seem to have denied that Jesus had a real body as early as the first century, for a few of the later writings of the New Testament allude to the issue. The author of 2 John, for example, warns his readers that "many deceivers have gone out into the world, who do not acknowledge that Jesus Christ came in flesh" (v. 7). John asserts in the prologue of his Gospel that "the *Logos* [Word] became flesh and lived among us" (John 1:14). Both 2 John and the Gospel of John were probably written in the last decade of the first century. In the early second century Ignatius warned against such views when he wrote to the Christians at Tralles in Asia Minor, "Do not listen whenever anyone speaks to you apart from Jesus Christ. Jesus descended from David's family, born of Mary. He truly was born, and ate, and drank. He was truly persecuted by Pontius Pilate, truly crucified and died, . . . and he was truly raised from the dead" (Ign. *Trall.* 9.1–2). Everything Ignatius mentions has to do with the physical nature of Jesus. It is a doctrinal statement defining one of the important boundaries about belief in Jesus Christ. He lived on this earth in a real body of flesh.

Polycarp, whom Irenaeus knew as a young man in Smyrna, raises the same issue in his letter *To the Philippians*:

> Whoever does not acknowledge that Jesus Christ has come in flesh is an antichrist, and whoever does not acknowledge the testimony of the cross belongs to the devil, and whoever crafts the sayings of the Lord to meet his own desires and says there is no resurrection or judgment is Satan's firstborn child. Therefore, let us forsake the folly of the many and their false teachings

---

Irenaeus on the Universal Belief of the Church

The church, although scattered throughout the whole world, ... has received from the apostles and their disciples the faith in one God the Father Almighty, "who made the heaven and the earth and the sea and everything in them [Acts 4:24]," and in one Christ Jesus, the Son of God, who was made flesh for our salvation, and in the Holy Spirit, who proclaimed through the prophets the ways of salvation and the coming of our beloved Christ Jesus the Lord and his birth from the virgin and his suffering and resurrection from the dead and his ascension into heaven in the flesh, and his return from heaven in the glory of the Father to "sum up all things" [Eph. 1:10] and to raise all human flesh so that "every knee might bow of things in heaven and on earth and under the earth and every tongue confess" [Phil. 2:10–11] to Christ Jesus our Lord and God and Savior and King according to the good pleasure of the invisible Father. ... The church, although scattered in the whole world, as we said previously, has received the message and this faith and carefully preserves it as if it lived in one house. ... The churches situated in Germany have not believed or handed on anything different, nor those in Spain or France, or those in the East, or in Egypt or Libya, or those situated in the mid-part of the world. ... Like the sun ... which is one and the same in the whole world, so too the light, the message of the truth, shines everywhere and enlightens all people who want to come to knowledge of the truth.

Irenaeus, *Against Heresies* 1.10.1, 2

---

and return to the doctrine that was handed down to us from the beginning. (Pol. *Phil.* 7.1–2)

The doctrines of the early Christians stated what they considered to be the truth about Jesus Christ. They marked the boundaries of what was acceptable and what was unacceptable to believe about him. It was not acceptable to believe that he was a divine being that lacked a real human body and, therefore, did not participate fully in the humanity that we humans know. As we will see in later chapters, it was also not acceptable to believe that his status was anything less than that of God himself.

By the end of the second century these doctrines about Jesus and God were being summarized in creed-like statements sometimes called the rule of faith, and sometimes called a baptismal confession because it would be repeated by a person about to be baptized. The doctrines contained in these statements of faith were considered to go back to the teachings of the apostles and to represent what Jesus Christ himself had taught them. They were believed to be found in the writings of the apostles in the Scriptures. It was this connection with Christ through the teachings of the apostles found in the Scriptures that gave authority to the doctrines accepted by the earliest Christians.

Classical Christian doctrine, as the phrase is used in this book, refers to those doctrines the church accepted in the first four centuries of its existence and gave expression to primarily in the Nicene Creed. These classical doctrines, which have defined the belief of the church from its most ancient days, are the doctrines surveyed in this book.

Points for Discussion

1. Define the term "doctrine" from your own understanding of the concept.
2. Do you think doctrine is important to the church? Why?
3. Do you think doctrine was important to the early Christians?
4. Collect as many statements from the New Testament as you are able that say something about doctrine. What do these statements teach us?
5. Does Jesus's question in Matthew 16:15 suggest anything about doctrine or its importance?

Resources for Further Reading

Heine, Ronald E. "What Is Christian Doctrine?" *Stone-Campbell Journal* 1, no. 1 (1998): 45–57.

McGrath, Alister E. *The Genesis of Doctrine*. Grand Rapids: Eerdmans; Vancouver, BC: Regent College Publishing, 1990. See ch. 6.

Oden, Thomas C. *The Rebirth of Orthodoxy*. San Francisco: HarperSanFrancisco, 2003. See chs. 3, 4, 9.

2

Christian Scripture

The Source of Classical Christian Doctrine

> Then he opened their mind to understand the
> scriptures.
>
> Luke 24:45

Identifying the Major Personalities

Polycarp: Bishop of Smyrna in the mid-second century and author of a letter to the Christians at Philippi.

Marcion: Christian teacher in the mid-second century who rejected Christian use of the Old Testament.

Justin Martyr: Christian apologist and teacher in Rome in the mid-second century; first to apply the term "Gospels" to Christian writings about Jesus.

Irenaeus: Bishop of Lyons, France, in the last quarter of the second century; first to refer to nearly all the writings of our New Testament.

Classical Christian doctrine is built on Scripture. All the chapters that follow in this book represent attempts of the early Christians to understand the teachings of the Scriptures. Our word "Scripture" is the translation, via the Latin language, of a Greek word that means "writing." But what were the Scriptures, or writings, that those early Christians were attempting to understand? We Christians of the twenty-first century have an automatic answer to that question. We can point to a copy of the Bible and say this is what they were interpreting. The most common usage of the word "Scripture" today is in reference to the book we label the Bible.[1] Scripture, in other words, refers to what Christians consider to be the authoritative book about Jesus and God's revelation in relation to him. But the answer to our question was not so automatic or obvious in the first few centuries of the Christian era. The early Christians had to wrestle with the question of what writings belonged in what we so easily refer to as Scripture.

I stated in the preface and again in chapter 1 that the doctrines discussed in this book are those that are represented in the Nicene Creed. There is, however, no statement of what constitutes Scripture in the Nicene Creed. Nor is there any ancient evidence suggesting that there was any discussion of this subject at the Council of Nicaea, which produced the creed. The main discussions about what would constitute Christian Scripture took place in the second and third centuries. These discussions occurred not in the context of church councils but in local debates about which books were appropriate for reading in the worship of the church or should be considered authoritative in determining Christian teaching. We have an example of such a local debate from the end of the second century in a letter of Serapion, bishop of Antioch, to the church in Rhossus, which lay not far northwest of Antioch. Serapion's office of bishop seems to have extended over Rhossus as well as Antioch. When Serapion visited the troubled church, he thought the division was over a dispute about whether a Gospel claiming to come from Peter could be read in the church. Not knowing the contents of this Gospel well, and assuming that the conflict was only about

---

1. "Scripture" may also be used to refer to the sacred writings of other religions.

reading it in the church, he said it could be read. Later, when he had read the Gospel carefully, he discovered that it contained false teachings about Christ. He then revoked the permission he had granted for the *Gospel of Peter* to be read in the church.[2] We will look at some broader-based discussions concerning Scripture in relation to crises in the second-century church in the sections that follow.

The earliest Christians derived their doctrine from Scripture. This does not mean, of course, that they did not interpret Scripture in presenting what they considered to be its teachings, or that they were not influenced by factors outside of Scripture in their interpretations. It is only to say that Scripture was the source from which they mined the ore of their doctrines. What we are looking at in this chapter is the development of the concept of Christian Scripture in the period preceding the Nicene Creed.

The Scriptures of the Earliest Christians

The writings that constitute what Christians today call the New Testament began to be composed perhaps as early as fifteen years after the death and resurrection of Jesus and continued to appear over the next fifty years.[3] They were not, however, usually considered to be Scripture in the first century of the Christian era.[4] The earliest Christians did not, therefore, have what we call the New Testament. Scripture for them meant the Hebrew Scriptures, which Christians today call the Old Testament. The Hebrew Scriptures were the authoritative books of the Jewish people. The first Christians used these books because they were Jews by birth. They believed that Jesus of Nazareth was the Jewish Messiah that they had anticipated on the basis of

2. This letter of Serapion is preserved in Eusebius, *Ecclesiastical History* 6.12.
3. This is based on the assumption that a few of Paul's letters may have appeared in the mid-40s and that the Johannine literature appeared in the mid-90s.
4. The one possible exception is the rather ambiguous statement about Paul's letters in 2 Pet. 3:15–16.

certain texts in the Hebrew Scriptures. They read the Hebrew Scriptures in a translation into the Greek language made years earlier by the Jewish community and used by Jews throughout the world who spoke Greek rather than Hebrew. This translation is called the Septuagint. It is what constituted Scripture for the first Christians. All references to Scripture in our New Testament are to what we today call the Old Testament.[5]

The Hebrew Scriptures have continued to be an essential part of Christian Scripture from the beginning of the church to the present day. The New Testament alone is not Christian Scripture. It is Old Testament plus New Testament that is Christian Scripture. The church has insisted on this combination ever since the books of the New Testament came to be considered a part of Christian Scripture. We will see in a later section in this chapter how the larger church in the second century rejected the attempt of a minority to discontinue the use of the Old Testament as Christian Scripture.

The Addition of Christian Writings to the Writings of the Hebrew Scriptures

The earliest Christians used the Scriptures of the Jewish community, but they did not read them as other members of the Jewish community read them. The law of Moses was the most important part of the Scriptures for the larger Jewish community. The Mosaic law, and its interpretations by the rabbis, directed the way the Jewish people lived. Christians, however, considered Christ to have been the fulfillment of the Hebrew Scriptures. For Christians, therefore, from the beginning these writings were useful primarily for what they could learn from them about Christ. A common Jewish objection to the Christian use of the Hebrew Scriptures was that Christians claimed to worship the God revealed in those writings, but they did

---

5. See Ronald E. Heine, *Reading the Old Testament with the Ancient Church* (Grand Rapids: Baker Academic, 2007), 31–46.

not keep the law, which was central to the Hebrew Scriptures.[6] Christians read the Hebrew Scriptures in the Greek translation, looking for teachings about or by Christ. The concluding chapter of Luke's Gospel indicates that Jesus himself taught his followers to read the Hebrew Scriptures in this way.[7] Throughout his ministry, Jesus had made his own teachings equal to those of Moses. His followers had heard him say, "You have heard that the ancients said. . . . But I say to you . . ."[8] All of the sayings that Jesus attributes to "the ancients" come from the law of Moses. Statements such as these by Jesus suggested that his teachings were on a par with, or even superseded, the teachings of Moses and the prophets as an authority for his followers.[9]

Jewish Objection to Christian Use of the Hebrew Scriptures

You [Christians] hope to gain something good from God although you do not keep his commands. Are you unaware that, "That soul which is not circumcised on the eighth day will be cut off from its generation" [Gen. 17:14]? . . . You, then, despise this covenant outright and neglect the things that follow, and still attempt to convince yourselves that you know God although you do none of the things those who fear God do.

Justin Martyr, *Dialogue with Trypho the Jew* 10.3–4

The message about Jesus was called the gospel ("good news") by the early Christians. It was the story of Jesus told by the apostles in their preaching. The apostles had been with Jesus and had seen his deeds and heard his teachings firsthand. They were eyewitnesses to the story of Jesus. There were, of course, other eyewitnesses to some of Jesus's activities and teachings. But these others were not on a par with the apostles as eyewitnesses, because the apostles were those closest followers who

6. Justin, *Dialogue with Trypho the Jew* 10.
7. See Luke 24:13–32, 44–48.
8. Matt. 5:21–22, 27–28, 31–32, 33–34, 38–39, 43–44.
9. See Denis M. Farkasfalvy, "The Early Development of the New Testament Canon," in *The Formation of the New Testament Canon*, by William R. Farmer and Denis M. Farkasfalvy (New York: Paulist Press, 1983), 97–178.

had been with him continually throughout his ministry. They, therefore, constituted the highest court of appeal when it came to authenticating what Jesus had done or said. When the words and deeds of Jesus began to be written down, it was natural for the Christians to treat these accounts as Scripture in the same way they treated the writings of Moses and the prophets.

Paul's writings are the earliest Christian writings that we possess. They contain hints of understandings among the early Christians that later resulted in their expanding what they considered to be Scripture beyond those writings that made up the Hebrew Scriptures. Paul recognized three sources of authority in his letters. First, of course, he recognized and used the Hebrew Scriptures as authority. He did not, however, use them to regulate how Christians should live, as the Jews used the law to define and regulate their lives. The main authority of the Hebrew Scriptures for Christians was the testimony they were understood to bear to Christ. Paul used them to validate his message about Jesus. In Romans 15:3–4, for example, he cites the words of Psalm 69:9 as descriptive of Jesus and says further, speaking of the Hebrew Scriptures in general, "For whatever was written in former days was written for *our* instruction" (NRSV; emphasis added). Second, Paul knew and used traditions about Jesus and sayings of Jesus as a source of authority. In his First Letter to the Corinthians he gives instructions about marriage based on a teaching of Jesus.[10] In other passages he grounds his instructions in traditions about Jesus that he has received from the other apostles.[11] Jesus's words, and events from his life recounted by the apostles, were considered a source of authority by Christians. Finally, Paul considered the office of apostle itself to carry authority. In the verses about marriage from 1 Corinthians 7 quoted in the sidebar, Paul carefully distinguishes the teaching of Jesus on the subject of marriage from what he himself says on a further matter about which he knows no teaching

10. 1 Cor. 7:10–11; cf. Mark 10:11–12; Luke 16:18.
11. 1 Cor. 15:1–11; see also 11:23–25.

> ### Paul's Distinction between His Own Words and the Lord's
>
> To those who are married I command, *actually not I but the Lord*, that a wife not be separated from her husband, but if she is already separated, let her remain unmarried or be reconciled to her husband, and that a husband not divorce his wife. Now to the rest, *it is I who speak, not the Lord*: If any brother has an unbelieving wife and she consents to live with him, let him not divorce her. And if any wife has an unbelieving husband and he consents to live with her, let her not divorce her husband.
>
> 1 Corinthians 7:10–13 (emphasis added)

of Jesus. But it is quite clear that he expects his own words, as those of an apostle, to carry authority as well.[12]

In his letters, then, Paul looked to the Hebrew Scriptures, to the sayings and story of Jesus, and to his own office of apostle as sources of authority. These three sources of authority suggest the shape that the Christian canon of Scripture later took: Hebrew Scriptures, Gospels, and writings of apostles.[13] This is not to suggest that Paul determined the shape of the later Christian canon. Paul's letters probably reflect general Christian understandings of authority that were afloat among the earliest Christians. From the beginning, the Christians looked to the story of Jesus and the teachings of the apostles as carrying authority in addition to the Hebrew Scriptures. The story of Jesus and the teachings of the apostles, however, were not yet in written form in the earliest days of the Christian community.

By the first half of the second century, the apostles were no longer living. Their letters to churches or individuals, along with their recollections of the story of Jesus as preserved either in their own words or in the writings of others, were widely known but had not yet been gathered into a single collection. In the Christian writings produced during this period, individual

---

12. 1 Cor. 7:12; see also 7:39–40.
13. Cf. François Bovon, "The Canonical Structure of Gospel and Apostle," in *Studies in Early Christianity* (Tübingen: Mohr Siebeck, 2003; repr., Grand Rapids: Baker Academic, 2005), 163–77.

> ### Early Citations of Unidentified Phrases from Apostolic Writings
>
> For everyone who does not confess that Jesus Christ has come in the flesh is antichrist [see 1 John 4:2–3], and whoever does not confess the testimony of the cross is of the devil [see 1 John 3:8]. Whoever perverts the sayings of the Lord to his own desires and says there is no resurrection or judgment is the firstborn of Satan. Therefore, let us forsake the vanity and false teachings of the multitudes and return to the word that was delivered to us from the beginning [see 1 John 1:1; 2:24], being sober in relation to prayers, and persevering in fasting [see 1 Pet. 4:7], entreating the God who sees all things not to bring us into temptation [see Matt. 6:13], as the Lord said. The spirit is willing, but the flesh is weak [see Matt. 26:41].
>
> Polycarp, *To the Philippians* 7

letters of Paul are sometimes referred to, but they are not yet cited as Scripture. In the letter known as *1 Clement*, written perhaps in the last decade of the first century and addressed to the Christians at Corinth, the author refers to a letter that Paul had written to them—our 1 Corinthians—and summarizes what Paul said in 1 Corinthians 1:12.[14] Likewise, Polycarp, in his letter *To the Philippians*, refers to Paul having written to them.[15] A number of phrases that clearly come from what we call the epistles in the New Testament can be found in the Christian literature written in the first half of the second century. These phrases are never introduced as Scripture, however, nor are they identified as coming from a letter of Paul, Peter, or John.[16] The writings of apostles were known in this period, but they were not yet considered to be on a par with the Hebrew Scriptures. It seems that the Gospels were the first to be recognized by the early Christians to be equal in authority to the Hebrew Scriptures. Justin, writing in the mid-second century in Rome, refers to the memoirs of the apostles, which, he says, are called

14. *1 Clem.* 47.1–3.
15. Pol. *Phil.* 11.3.
16. The passages from *1 Clement* and Polycarp discussed above are exceptions to this statement.

Gospels. He states that these are read, along with the writings of the Hebrew prophets, in the worship assemblies of the church.[17] By the end of the second century nearly all the writings of our New Testament can be found cited by Irenaeus and Tertullian.[18]

Two Challenges to the Apostolic Faith in the Second Century

The church faced two crises in the second century that threatened to turn Christian faith in directions different from those it had taken based on the teachings of the apostles. These threats came from gnosticism and Marcionism. The rise of the latter can be dated with some precision. The date of the rise of gnosticism is ambiguous. I will treat gnosticism first, as it most likely was the earlier of the two threats to what came to be known as orthodox Christian faith.

The Gnostics and a Different Jesus

Sometime in the mid-second century it became important to the church to define which writings about Jesus should be accepted and used as the authoritative statements about his life and teachings. Various subgroups of Christians had formed around teachers who had either composed a Gospel or accepted Gospels other than the four accepted by the wider church. Modern scholars have labeled these subgroups gnostics, which is from the Greek word meaning "knowers."[19] Gnostics believed that they were in possession of secret knowledge about deity and the meaning of human life. Some of the Gospels used by the gnostics said nothing about Jesus's death and resurrection; some denied

17. Justin, *1 Apology* 66.3; 67.3.
18. The only writings in our New Testament that cannot be found in Irenaeus are James, Jude, 2 Peter, and 3 John.
19. For a brief survey of some basic beliefs of the gnostics, see Michael Allen Williams, *Rethinking "Gnosticism"* (Princeton: Princeton University Press, 1996), 7–28. Gnostic Gospels in English translation can be found in *The Nag Hammadi Scriptures*, ed. Marvin Meyer (New York: HarperCollins, 2007).

that he had had a physical body; one even made Judas a hero rather than a villain in his betrayal of Jesus. The teachings and writings of the gnostics made the church aware of its need to define what constituted a valid description of the life and work of Jesus and what did not. A major criterion that arose during the time of the gnostic crisis has been called the criterion of apostolicity. This rather daunting phrase means simply that any teaching claiming to come from Jesus or to be about Jesus must have as its source either an apostle or an immediate disciple of an apostle. It would be too much to say that the gnostic crisis of the mid-second century caused the church to decide which writings would constitute the collection that would define the acceptable description of Jesus and his teachings. The crisis was, however, a factor in moving the church in that direction.

Marcion and the Rejection of the Christian Use of the Old Testament

The time of Marcion's activities can be dated rather precisely. He was excommunicated by the church in Rome in AD 144 for his heretical teachings. After this he formed his own group of Christians.[20] His significance for our discussion is that he argued that the church could not use the Hebrew Scriptures. They were addressed, he argued, only to the Jewish people. He believed that Jesus of Nazareth had been not the Jewish Messiah sent by the God of the Old Testament but the son of a God unknown until the appearance of Jesus in the fifteenth year of Tiberius Caesar, as Luke identifies the date of Jesus's baptism in the third chapter of his Gospel. Marcion thought that only what the apostle Paul taught could be trusted, and even some of Paul's writings, he feared, had been tampered with by Jewish-leaning Christians. In the absence of the Hebrew Scriptures to define and support the Christian message about Jesus, Marcion drew up a list of works that would be recognized as authoritative in his churches. This list contained the Gospel of Luke, which Marcion edited by

20. For a brief survey of Marcion, see Heine, *Reading the Old Testament*, 70–73.

> ### Marcion on the Identity of Christ
>
> Marcion has laid down the position that the Christ, revealed in the days of Tiberius for the salvation of all nations, was from a previously unknown god. He is a different being than the one who has been appointed by God the creator for the restoration of the Jewish state. This latter is yet to come. Between these two beings he interposes the separation of a great and absolute difference. It is as great a difference as that between what is just and what is good, or between the law and the gospel. In short it is as great as the difference between Judaism and Christianity.
>
> Tertullian, *Against Marcion* 4.6; *ANF* 3:351 (translation modified)

removing certain sections, and ten letters of Paul, also edited in places: Galatians, 1 and 2 Corinthians, Romans, 1 and 2 Thessalonians, Ephesians, Colossians, Philemon, and Philippians.[21]

The larger body of Christians disagreed with Marcion on three major points regarding his views on the sacred writings of the church. First and foremost, they disagreed with him about the Christian use of the Hebrew Scriptures. These, as we saw above, constituted the entirety of Christian Scripture in the earliest period of the church, and they had continued to be the highest written authority recognized in the church. This treasure of what was considered to be testimony about Jesus could not and would not be jettisoned by the church. Second, Marcion recognized only one Gospel. While we do not have any listings from the church as early as the time of Marcion, in just a few years, before the end of the second century, the larger church would insist that there are four Gospels, no more and no fewer. Finally, Marcion recognized the teachings of only one apostle. The church recognized the teachings of at least three: Matthew, John, and Paul (and Peter).[22] Again, it would be too much to say

21. Marcion's works are all lost. We derive most of our information about him from Tertullian's large treatise *Against Marcion*, which can be found in vol. 3 of *The Ante-Nicene Fathers*.

22. The authorship of 2 Peter, especially, was questioned by some early Christians.

Irenaeus on the Four Gospels

The Gospels can be neither more in number nor fewer than they are. For because there are four inhabited regions of the world, and four general winds, and the church is scattered over the whole earth, and the gospel is the pillar and foundation of the church and the breath of its life, consequently the church must have four pillars exhaling immortality from every quarter and making people live. Therefore, it is clear that the Logos, the maker of all things "who sits upon the cherubim" and holds all things together, has given us the gospel in fourfold form, but held together by the one Spirit. David, when requesting his presence, says, "You who sit upon the cherubim, appear" [Ps. 80:2]. For the cherubim have four faces and their faces are images of the activity of the Son of God. "The first animal," it says, "is like a lion," emphasizing his effectiveness, leadership, and kingly office. "And the second was like a calf," pointing to his ceremonial and priestly position. "The third had the face of a person," which clearly indicates his coming as a human being. "The fourth was like an eagle flying," which reveals the gift of the Spirit hovering over the church [see Rev. 4:7]. The Gospels, therefore, on which Christ is seated, are in harmony with these beings. For the Gospel according to John relates his authoritative and highly esteemed generation from the Father, . . . and that according to Luke, since he bears a priestly stamp, begins with Zacharias the priest making an offering to God. . . . The Gospel according to Matthew announces his birth as a human when it says, "The book of the generation of Jesus Christ, son of David, son of Abraham" [Matt. 1:1]. And that according to Mark begins from the prophetic Spirit . . . when it says, "The beginning of the gospel, as it is written in Isaiah the prophet" [Mark 1:1].

Irenaeus, *Against Heresies* 3.11.8

---

that Marcion's teachings caused the church to draw up its own list of acceptable writings. He must, however, have caused the church to think seriously about the growing need for such a list.

The Concept of Canon and the Writings of the New Testament

I have already used the term "canon" a few times in this chapter. It comes from a Greek word meaning "a standard or rule for measuring." To illustrate its meaning I sometimes ask two or three students to go to the board and draw a line they think is twelve inches long. The lines always differ from one another in length. Then I ask how we can know which, if any, of the three lines is actually twelve inches long. I take out a ruler, of course, and point out that we do not have to guess how long a line of twelve inches is. There is a recognized standard that we can put alongside the lines to see if they are too long, too short, or exactly correct. This is the implicit concept of a canon. It is a standard that allows one to judge whether something is correct or incorrect. The New Testament canon is the collection of writings judged by the Christians of the first two centuries to depict accurately the life and teachings of Jesus. The primary basis for inclusion in the canon was the proximity of the various authors of the documents to Jesus himself. Apostles were best because they had been eyewitnesses of the events and had heard the teachings. The chain of authority could not reach any further away than immediate disciples of apostles. They had, at least, known the eyewitnesses and had heard their teachings.

We have a list of recognized New Testament writings that dates probably from the end of the second century and, in all probability, derives from the church in Rome. It is called the Muratorian Canon, named after the man who discovered it in a library in Europe in the eighteenth century. The beginning of the document is missing. The first book mentioned is Luke, which is referred to as the third of the Gospels. Presumably Matthew and Mark had been mentioned in the missing part. John's Gospel is called the fourth, followed by the Acts of the Apostles. Next comes a presentation of the Pauline epistles. Paul is said to have written to only seven churches by name: the Corinthians, Ephesians, Philippians, Colossians, Galatians, Thessalonians, and Romans. The author notes that there are two letters to the Corinthians and to the Thessalonians. Paul also wrote to Philemon, to Titus, and twice to Timothy. Next the fragment says there are two forged Pauline letters, one to the Laodiceans and another to the Alexandrians. These forgeries are attributed to the Marcionite heresy. It adds that there were many additional letters that the church did not accept. The letter of Jude and two letters of John are also said to be accepted, as are the Wisdom of Solomon and the apocalypses of John and Peter, though the author adds that he and others prefer the latter not to be read in the church. The Christian writing known as *The Shepherd* is also said to be rejected because of its recent authorship. The fragment closes with a list of heretics whose works are rejected.[23]

No church council made an official pronouncement about the New Testament canon until the Council of Trent in the sixteenth century, but the list of books recognized as authoritative for Christian teaching had been consistent since at least the end of the second century.[24] These writings, along with the Hebrew Scriptures, constitute Christian Scripture. These are the texts that were discussed and interpreted by the early Christians in arriving at the doctrines presented in this book.

Points for Discussion

1. List some ways in which what the first Christians considered to be their Scriptures differs from what you consider to be Scripture today.
2. How does the collection of books recognized today as Christian Scripture reflect traces of viewpoints already present in the writings of Paul?
3. What is the most basic and important concept belonging to the idea of canon?

23. The Muratorian Canon can be read in Daniel J. Theron, *Evidence of Tradition* (Grand Rapids: Baker, 1980), 106–13; also see §103 in *A New Eusebius: Documents Illustrating the History of the Church to AD 337*, ed. J. Stevenson and W. H. C. Frend (Grand Rapids: Baker Academic, forthcoming). An alternative, later date for the Muratorian Canon has been proposed by A. C. Sundberg Jr. in "Canon Muratori: A Fourth-Century List," *Harvard Theological Review* 66 (1973): 1–41.

24. Lists and discussions of acceptable and unacceptable books for use in the church from the first half of the fourth century can be read in Eusebius, *Ecclesiastical History* 3.3.1–5 and 3.25.1–7 (§289 in *A New Eusebius*) and in Athanasius, Letter 39. The latter can be found in *NPNF*, 2nd series, 4:551–52.

4. Provide a list of factors that seem to have convinced Christians in the second century of the need to draw up a list of recognized books to be used in the church.

Resources for Further Reading

Farkasfalvy, Denis. "The Early Development of the New Testament Canon." In *The Formation of the New Testament Canon*, by William R. Farmer and Denis M. Farkasfalvy, 97–178. New York: Paulist Press, 1983.

Grant, R. M. "The New Testament Canon." In *The Cambridge History of the Bible*, edited by P. R. Ackroyd and C. F. Evans, 1:284–308. Cambridge: Cambridge University Press, 1970.

Heine, Ronald E. *Reading the Old Testament with the Ancient Church*. Grand Rapids: Baker Academic, 2007. See especially 31–74.

Irenaeus. *Against Heresies*. In *ANF*, vol. 1. Also available at http://www.ccel.org/fathers.html.

Justin Martyr. *First Apology*. In *ANF*, vol. 1. Also available at http://www.ccel.org/fathers.html.

Wilken, Robert Louis. *The Spirit of Early Christian Thought*. New Haven: Yale University Press, 2003. See especially 50–79.

Williams, Michael A. *Rethinking "Gnosticism."* Princeton: Princeton University Press, 1996. See especially 7–28.

3

"The Lord Our God Is One"

The Jewish God and the Christian Faith

Hear, Israel, the Lord our God is one Lord.

Deuteronomy 6:4

Identifying the Major Sources

Old Testament: The Hebrew Scriptures of the Jewish people, used as the Bible by the earliest Christians.

New Testament: The earliest preserved Christian documents, dating from the middle to the end of the first century AD.

The Apostolic Fathers: Writings of the second and third generations of Christians, dating from the first quarter of the second century AD through the middle of that century. These writings include the *Didache*, the first and second letters of Clement, the seven letters of Ignatius, the letter of Barnabas, the letter of Polycarp to the Philippians, and the *Shepherd of Hermas*.

All early Christian creeds begin with an affirmation of belief in God. Most of them, as with the Nicene Creed, state that the belief is in "one God."[1] So this book begins by examining this

1. The Apostles' Creed says only, "We believe in God . . ."

24

The Nicene Creed

We believe in one God, the Father almighty, maker of heaven and earth, of all things visible and invisible.

And in one Lord Jesus Christ, the only begotten Son of God, begotten by the Father before all ages, God from God, light from light, true God from true God, begotten, not made, of the same substance with the Father, through whom all things came to be, who, because of us humans and because of our salvation, came down from heaven and was made flesh by the Holy Spirit and the virgin Mary, and became incarnate, who was crucified for us under Pontius Pilate, and suffered and was buried, and was raised on the third day in accordance with the Scriptures, and who ascended into heaven and is seated at the right hand of the Father, and is coming again with glory to judge the living and the dead, whose kingdom will not end.

And [we believe] in the Holy Spirit, the Lord and life-giver, who proceeds from the Father, who is worshiped and glorified with the Father and the Son, who spoke through the prophets.

[And we believe] in one holy catholic and apostolic church; we confess one baptism for the forgiveness of sins; we anticipate the resurrection of the dead and the life of the age to come. Amen.

---

early Christian belief in one God. This chapter will look at the relation of the early Christian doctrine of the one God to the ancient Hebrew faith revealed in the Old Testament, focusing on the continuity between the Hebrew and the Christian doctrines. The following chapters will discuss ways in which the Christian doctrine of one God diverged from that of the Hebrews as the early Christians began to reflect on the divine nature of the Son and the Holy Spirit. The discussion will progress more or less chronologically, beginning with the literature of the Old and New Testaments and Apostolic Fathers in this chapter. The succeeding chapters look at the teaching about God in the Christian literature from the mid-second through the fourth centuries.

Many give little thought today to the idea that there is only one God. It has been assumed so long in our Western culture under the influence of the church that we do not consider the possibility that there might be many gods. The more usual question asked today is if God exists at all. Very few people at the time that Christianity arose questioned the existence of gods. What they questioned was the assertion that there was only one God. In the first few centuries of the church's existence the majority of the population assumed that there were many gods and worshiped a diversity of gods. The belief of Jews and Christians that there was only one God sounded strange to most people. The early Christians often had to defend their belief in one God. The doctrine also caused them problems. Their non-Christian neighbors attributed the control of everything from weather conditions to their personal success in business or military campaigns to the various gods. When they noticed that the Christians were not present at public festivals honoring these gods, they feared that the gods would be angry and that the whole community would be punished by flood, famine, disease, or some other natural catastrophe. This was sometimes the reason for local persecutions of Christians. When the emperor demanded that all citizens offer a pinch of incense to an image of himself, Christians refused because they understood this to mean recognizing him as another god. Roman government officials interpreted this refusal to offer incense to an image of the emperor as a sign of disloyalty to the state on the part of Christians. This was another factor that sometimes led to persecution of Christians. The doctrine of the one God was very important to the early Christians. Some of them died rather than compromise it.

The Doctrine of the One God in the Old Testament

The Old Testament begins with the story of God creating the heavens, the earth, and everything contained in them. There are several creation stories in ancient literature. Some of them have approximately the same order of creation as that found in the first chapter of Genesis. The difference is that in Genesis the creation proceeds from one God. All other stories involve a plurality of gods and preexisting material from which things are made. In Genesis God creates by speaking or commanding, "Let there be . . ." There is no preexisting material explicitly mentioned. Everything comes into being from the power of God's word alone. The creation story is of great importance for later Christian theology.[2] One of the important conclusions that later theology based (at least partially) on the creation story is that God alone exists without beginning. Everything else is created by him and has a beginning.

The next major event recorded in the Old Testament, so far as the story of the one God is concerned, is the calling of Abraham in Genesis 12:1–3. God chooses Abraham, establishes a special relationship with him, and makes some very long-range promises to him. The story of Abraham explains why the Hebrews came to call this God who created the universe *their* God. In choosing Abraham, God was in effect choosing a people through whom he would work and reveal himself. The Hebrew people were the descendants of Abraham through his son Isaac and Isaac's son Jacob. Later writers in the Old and New Testaments often identify God as the God of Abraham, Isaac, and Jacob, or the God of the fathers, meaning these three men.

The story that unfolds from Exodus through the end of the Old Testament is the story of God's relationship with and actions for these descendants of Abraham. The most outstanding of these actions is God's deliverance of the Hebrews from slavery in the exodus from Egypt. This event became fundamental to the later Hebrew religion and was remembered and celebrated each year in the feast of the Passover. God also gave the Hebrew people their law. This law is based on the assumption that he alone is God, and that it is he alone who has provided for them, especially by delivering them from slavery in Egypt.[3] The words of Deuteronomy 6:4, known as the *Shema* from the first Hebrew word in the statement ("Hear"), became the foundational belief of the Hebrew people: "Hear, Israel, the Lord our God is one

2. This will be discussed in ch. 10.
3. See Exod. 20:1–6 and Deut. 6:4.

The God of the Hebrews Alone Is God

To whom then will you liken God, or what likeness compare with him? An idol?—a workman casts it, and a goldsmith overlays it with gold, and casts for it silver chains. . . . Have you not known? Have you not heard? . . . It is he who sits above the circle of the earth, and its inhabitants are like grasshoppers; who stretches out the heavens like a curtain, and spreads them like a tent to live in; who brings princes to naught, and makes the rulers of the earth as nothing. . . . To whom then will you compare me, or who is my equal? says the Holy One. Lift up your eyes on high and see: Who created these? He who brings out their host and numbers them, calling them all by name; because he is great in strength, mighty in power, not one is missing. . . . Have you not known? Have you not heard? The Lord is the everlasting God, the Creator of the ends of the earth. He does not faint or grow weary; his understanding is unsearchable.

Isaiah 40:18–28 (NRSV)

Lord." Jesus later cited this verse as the most important of all the commandments (Mark 12:29–30).

Although God revealed himself to the Hebrew people as the one and only God from the beginning, they often turned away from him to the many gods of their pagan neighbors. This aspect of the relationship between the one God and the Hebrew people is the theme that structures the book of Judges.[4] The later prophets of Israel sometimes spoke of God as Israel's husband and Israel as an unfaithful wife. These prophets understood the captivity of Israel by Assyria, and later, the captivity of Judah by Babylon, to be due to the people's unfaithfulness to the one God.[5]

The preaching recorded in the second half of the book of Isaiah puts a special emphasis on proclaiming the doctrine of the one God. Isaiah attributes the return of the Hebrews from the Babylonian exile and the restoration to their homeland to the work of God. It was the Persian king Cyrus who made it possible for the Hebrews to return to Palestine after he had conquered Babylon, but Isaiah asserts that Cyrus was the instrument

---

4. See an example of this theme in Judg. 3:7–11.
5. See Jer. 2:1–3:11 and Hosea 4.

used by God to achieve this goal.[6] In Isaiah 44–45, where the prophet relates the forthcoming restoration of the Hebrews to their homeland, he recalls God's creation of the nation of Israel by the choosing of Abraham and then asserts that it was this same God who had created the heavens and earth. The entire history of the Hebrew people had been in the hands of the one God, creator of heaven and earth.

After the return from the Babylonian exile the Hebrews never again turned away from the God of Abraham, Isaac, and Jacob. Faith in this one God became the most characteristic feature of the Jewish people. The Romans even granted the Jews the right, in most cases, to live by their own laws because of their strong belief that there was only one God. They were known as the people of the one God who had created heaven and earth.

The Doctrine of the One God in the New Testament

The earliest Christians were all Jews or Jewish proselytes. They saw faith in Jesus not as a new religion but as the fulfillment of promises that had been made to the Hebrew people in the Old Testament. In Acts 2 the author presents a sermon by the apostle Peter as the first general proclamation about Jesus after his crucifixion and resurrection. This sermon is delivered in the Jewish temple in Jerusalem to a group of Jews from all over the Mediterranean world who had come to Jerusalem to celebrate the Jewish festival of Pentecost. Peter addresses them as a Jew speaking to Jews. He preaches about the Jew Jesus of Nazareth. What he says about Jesus is grounded in the doctrine of the one God of the Old Testament. This God has put his stamp of approval on Jesus by the mighty deeds that he performed among them. It was the plan of this God that Jesus be handed over to them and crucified. It was this God who raised Jesus from the dead. Jesus has now been exalted to the right hand of this

6. See Isa. 44–45.

29

God, and this "God has made him both Lord and Messiah."[7] Peter's sermon is a message about Jesus, but it would be nothing without the one God of the Old Testament.

The Old Testament doctrine of the one God, who chose the fathers Abraham, Isaac, and Jacob and revealed himself to their descendants, is foundational to the earliest Christian faith. Jesus cites the *Shema* from Deuteronomy 6:4 as the most important of all commandments (Mark 12:28–30). James 2:19 shows that the acceptance of the *Shema* was assumed among Christians. To be Christian was to believe that God is one. The doctrine of the one God was the basis of the missionary preaching of Paul to the Gentiles.[8] Statements concerning faith in one God recur throughout the New Testament.[9] He is often recognized as the creator God of Genesis 1.[10] When the earliest Christians spoke of the one God, they did not mean some God different from the God of the Old Testament. They meant the one and the same God who had created the universe, chosen Abraham, delivered the Hebrews from slavery in the exodus, brought them back from Babylonian exile, and now, they believed, revealed himself in Jesus of Nazareth. The Christians often identified him in the New Testament in the same way the Hebrews had done, as the God of Abraham, Isaac, and Jacob[11] or, in a phrase that meant the same thing, as the God of the fathers.[12]

The Doctrine of the One God in the Apostolic Fathers

The small collection of literature referred to as the Apostolic Fathers was all, with one exception, addressed to churches or

7. Acts 2:22–36 (NRSV); quote from 2:36.

8. See 1 Thess. 1:8–9; Acts 14:15; 17:22–28.

9. See 1 Cor. 8:4–6; Eph. 4:6; Gal. 3:20; Rom. 3:29–30; 1 Tim. 2:5. God is sometimes referred to as the only God, as in Rom. 16:27; 1 Tim. 1:17; 6:15; Jude 25; John 17:3.

10. See Rom. 11:36; Heb. 2:10; Rev. 4:11, and, more directly, Acts 4:24; 14:15; 17:24; Rev. 10:6; 14:7.

11. See Acts 3:13; 7:32; Matt. 22:32; Mark 12:26; Luke 20:37.

12. See Acts 3:13; 5:30; 22:14.

An Early Christian Version of the Jewish *Shema*

On the subject of eating food that has been offered to idols, we know that idols are nothing in the world, and that there is no God but one. For even if there are so-called gods in heaven or on earth, as indeed there are many gods and lords, for us there is one God the Father, from whom all things come and we are in him, and one Lord Jesus Christ through whom all things come, and we are through him.

1 Corinthians 8:4–6

---

leaders of churches.[13] The doctrine of the one God continues along the same lines we observed above in the New Testament. When God is referred to in this literature, he is the God who revealed himself to the Hebrew people in the Old Testament. There are no arguments attempting to prove that there is only one God or that Christians believe in the one God of the Old Testament. It is clear, however, that the authors all assume this doctrine and that the people addressed hold this doctrine. When the author of *1 Clement*, for example, wants to argue against the divisions in the church at Corinth to which he is writing, he asks the rhetorical question, "Do we not have one God, and one Christ, and one Spirit of grace?" (*1 Clem.* 46.6). Here, of course, Christ and the Holy Spirit are mentioned simultaneously with the one God. This multiplicity, however, is not yet a problem in the thinking of the church regarding the doctrine of the one God any more than it has been in the literature of the New Testament, where, along with statements about God, statements are made about the divine nature of Jesus, who is said to be exalted to the right hand of God. In another context Clement assumes the God of the Christians to be the creator God of the Old Testament when he urges his readers to give their attention to "the Father and creator of the whole world" (*1 Clem.* 19.2).

13. The *Epistle to Diognetus* is addressed to someone who is not already a Christian.

Ignatius on the One God

The divine prophets lived in accordance with Jesus Christ. They were persecuted because they were inspired by his grace to convince the unbelievers that there is one God who has made himself known through Jesus Christ his Son. He is his Word proceeding from silence, who completely pleased the one who sent him.

Ignatius, *To the Magnesians* 8.2

The doctrine of the one God is often referred to in this literature in connection with his commandments, which are to be obeyed. The author of the *Didache* joins a reference to God as creator with the statement of Deuteronomy 6:5, and says that the first commandment for one following the way of life is to love "the God who made you" (*Did.* 1.2). The author of the *Epistle of Barnabas* makes a similar statement when he says, "You shall love the one who made you and fear the one who formed you" (*Barn.* 19.2). Finally, the author of the *Shepherd of Hermas* describes a modified version of the Hebrew *Shema*, joined with a statement about God as creator, as the first element of Christian faith. "First believe," he says, "that God is one, who created and ordered all things, and made all things exist out of what did not exist" (*Herm. Mand.* 1.1).

The literature and thought surveyed in this chapter come from approximately the first one hundred years of the church's life, from AD 40 to 150. The authors of this literature do not usually reflect on the doctrine of God or even argue for it. They simply assume it. But it was an assumption with far-reaching consequences. For one thing, it bound Judaism and Christianity together in continuity regarding the foundational doctrine of each religion. When the earliest Christians spoke of one God, they meant the God of the Old Testament, who had revealed himself to Israel and had given Israel the law. The doctrine of the one God could also have painful consequences when it became the basis of the persecution of Christians.

Philosophical concepts of God are largely absent from this literature of the first one hundred years of Christianity. We will see in the next chapter, however, how philosophy became important to many Christians at a slightly later period in their efforts to understand and defend the doctrine of the one God. We will also see how these philosophical concepts altered the Christian understanding of God.

Points for Discussion

1. What similarities do you see between the statement about belief in God in the Nicene Creed and (1) in the *Shema*, (2) in the New Testament, (3) in the Apostolic Fathers?
2. What do these similarities suggest?
3. Why do you think Peter says so much about God in his sermon about Jesus in Acts 2?
4. How is the *Shema* used in passages such as 1 Corinthians 8:4; James 2:19; and Mark 12:29?

Resources for Further Reading

Isaiah 45–46

1 Corinthians 8:4–6

Chadwick, Henry. *The Early Church*. Harmondsworth: Penguin, 1985. See especially 9–31.

Hall, Stuart G. *Doctrine and Practice in the Early Church*. Grand Rapids: Eerdmans, 1991. See especially 1–13.

4

"And the Word Was God"

The Christian Faith and the Greek Philosophers

In the beginning was the Word, and the Word
was with God, and the Word was God.

John 1:1

Identifying the Major Personalities

Heraclitus: A Greek philosopher of the sixth century BC who is considered to be the first to use the term *logos* in a philosophical manner.

Apologists of the second century: Christians who wrote defenses of the Christian faith to help non-Christians understand Christianity. These included Justin Martyr and Theophilus, who wrote in Greek and lived in the mid-second century AD, and Tertullian, who wrote in Latin at the end of the second century and early in the third century.

Stoics: Members of a school of philosophy taking its name from the Stoia, the name of the place in Athens where it met for discussions. It was started about 300 BC by a man named Zeno.

Middle Platonists: Greek philosophers of the first and second centuries AD who were disciples of Plato's philosophy but had modified it considerably by bringing in teachings from other schools of philosophy.

How can Christians say that God is one and, at the same time, claim that the Son is divine? This question began to bother thoughtful Christians at least as early as the second century. In this chapter we consider one of the early attempts made to answer this question. A few who claimed faith in Jesus in the second century were philosophers. They believed that the Greek concept of *logos* provided an answer to the question of the relationship of the Son to the Father. The Greek word *logos* can mean "reason"—that is, thought—or it can mean "speech"—that is, verbally expressed thought. Thought is private and internal to a person. Speech makes thought external and no longer the private possession of the person in whom it originates. *Logos* carried both of these connotations. In the New Testament it is usually translated with the English noun "word," as in the opening verses of John's Gospel. We begin by briefly sketching the use of the term *logos* by some significant Greek philosophers whose thought influenced early Christian thinkers either directly or indirectly. After this sketch, we will then look at how this philosophical concept was used to attempt to understand the relationship between God the Father and God the Son.

The Greek Philosophical Teaching about the *Logos*

If one had to choose a single word to sum up the ancient Greek way of understanding the world and existence, *logos* would be one of the top contenders for that honor. It is a word that embraces an ordered, rational way of perceiving things. The early Greek philosopher Heraclitus, who lived in the sixth century BC, used the term to describe the rational principle that maintained order in the universe. Though he thought most people were ignorant of this *logos* that ordered the universe and their own lives, it was, nevertheless, the *logos* that made it possible for them to understand both themselves and their world.

In the classical philosophy of Plato and Aristotle, *logos* refers primarily to the human *reasoning process*, or to the *reasoned speech* of human beings. Aristotle says that humans are the only animals to which nature gave *logos*.[1] It was the later Platonic philosophers and the Stoic philosophers, however, who had the greater influence on Christian thinkers who applied this concept to Christ.

Zeno, one of the founders of Stoicism, understood the universe to consist of an active part and a passive part. The passive part was matter; the active was *logos*, or god. The Stoics taught that *logos* was a part of everything in the universe. They called it the generative principle of the universe. Its action on the passive material was the cause of everything that exists. The rationality that human souls possess was thought to be a spark or seed from this rational principle called *logos*. This spark or seed that humans possess was thought to be what made it possible for humans to understand the world and to understand how they ought to live in the world. The Greek term *logos*, as noted above, could mean either the internal activity of thinking or the external expression of that thought in speech.

The disciples of Plato in this period, who are often called Middle Platonists today, combined teachings from the philosophy of the Stoics with the thought of Plato. It is their combination of these Stoic teachings about the *logos* with some of Plato's views that was used by the Christian apologists of the second century to express their understanding of the relationship of the Son of God to God the Father. Plato believed that there was a supreme principle, which he called "the Good" or "the One." This principle was purely intellectual and was totally transcendent. The latter meant that it was inaccessible in any direct way to human beings and could not be directly involved in material things. Plato had difficulty in showing how there could be any relationship between this highest principle and the created world. He suggested that there was a "Demiurge,"

---

1. Aristotle, *Politics* 1.2 (1253a 9f).

> ### Numenius on the First and Second God
>
> [I]t is not at all becoming that the First God should be the Creator; also the First God must be regarded as the father of the God who is Creator of the world.
>
> Numenius, quoted in Eusebius, *Preparation for the Gospel* 18.6; in Eusebius, *Preparation for the Gospel*, trans. E. H. Gifford (Grand Rapids: Baker, 1981), 2:580

which is a Greek term that means "creator," which operated as a kind of go-between for the highest principle and the creation. It was this Demiurge that caused the actual creation of the material universe.

The Middle Platonists adopted the Stoic concept of the divine *logos* that interacts with matter and creates, and they identified it with Plato's Demiurge or Creator. They, therefore, had a first God, the Good or the One of Plato, who was purely intellectual and had no direct relationship with anything outside himself. They also had a second, creator god, who could also be called the *logos*, whom they identified with Plato's Demiurge. This second god, or *logos*, was the creator of the material realm. Numenius, a Middle Platonist of the second century AD, refers to a first and a second God several times in the fragments that have been preserved from his writings.[2]

Philo, the first-century Jewish philosopher who influenced many early Christian teachers, stood in this Middle Platonic tradition. He did not call the creator a second God, but he used the term *logos*. He understood God to be transcendent and related to the world only by means of the *logos*. Philo understood the *logos* to be God's thoughts and, as such, a part of God himself. In the mind of God, the *logos* was something like a blueprint for the creation. But remember that *logos* could be thought expressed in speech as well as the internal working of

---

2. The fragments are found in Eusebius, *Preparation for the Gospel* 11.18 (537b); in Eusebius, *Praeparatio evangelica (Preparation for the Gospel)*, trans. E. H. Gifford (Grand Rapids: Baker, 1981), 2:580.

> ### The *Logos* in the Gospel of John
>
> In the beginning was the *Logos*, and the *Logos* was with God, and the *Logos* was God. He was in the beginning with God. All things were made through him, and not one thing was made without him.
>
> John 1:1–3

the mind. Philo applied this aspect of *logos* much as the Stoics had. As the expressed thought of God, the *logos* is exterior to God himself and is present in what is created. In this stage the *logos* is the expressed thought of God and no longer abides in the mind of God but is external to God and is present, like in Stoicism, in the object of its creative activity. Philo compares creation to an architectural process. First, the plan of a city takes shape in the mind of the architect; then he produces an external plan of the city that becomes the actual city. Philo never, however, attributes an actual body or personality to the *logos*.

The author of the Gospel of John applied the noun *logos* to Christ. This, in a sense, paved the way for the later Christian *Logos* theology of the second and third centuries. No one knows, however, whether in his prologue John had in mind this Greek philosophical tradition or some other background, such as the "word of the Lord" in the Old Testament. Most New Testament scholars today would probably not opt for this philosophical tradition as the background of John's thought. In the second century, however, this philosophical tradition is definitely and consciously employed in the attempt to understand the nature of Christ and his relation to God. When the early Christian theologians began to use the *logos* concept of Christ, they clearly chose a concept that would catch the attention of the Greek intellectual world and open up a multiplicity of possibilities for understanding Christ. Some of these possibilities would prove to be positive, and others negative. It was the idea of a first and second God connected with the use of the *logos* concept in Christian theology, for example, that

---

Justin Martyr's Belief in One God

There will never be another God ... nor was there from eternity ... except the one who made and ordered this universe. Nor do we think that our God is one, and yours another, but that there is [only] that very one who brought your fathers out of Egypt.... Nor have we hoped in any other, for there is no other, but in this God in whom also you hope, the God of Abraham, Isaac, and Jacob.

Justin Martyr, *Dialogue with Trypho the Jew* 11.1

---

prompted some early Christians to accuse *Logos* theologians of worshiping two Gods.

Justin Martyr and Second-Century *Logos* Theology

Most of the things said about Justin Martyr in this section were common to a group of writers of the third quarter of the second century whom we call the apologists, especially Athenagoras, Theophilus, and Tatian. I focus on Justin because his is the earliest and most complete exposition of the *Logos* theology among the apologists. Justin came to Christianity from a strong philosophical background. He tells of moving from one philosophical school to another in his search for the truth in the introduction to his *Dialogue with Trypho the Jew*. He began with the Stoics, then tried the philosophy of Aristotle as taught by Aristotle's followers called the peripatetics. From there he went to the Pythagoreans, and last, before becoming a follower of Christ, he tried the Platonists. Some think this description of his intellectual pilgrimage is a literary convention and not an account of his actual experience. Whether this was the case or not, his works show that he was well acquainted with the philosophies of his time, and he seems to have considered himself a philosopher throughout his career as a Christian.[3] It was natural that Justin would perceive the Christian faith through

---

3. See Eusebius, *Ecclesiastical History* 4.11.

> ## Justin Martyr on God's Transcendence
>
> Whenever my God says, "God went up from Abraham [Gen. 17:22]," or, "The Lord spoke to Moses [Exod. 6:28]," and, "The Lord went down to see the tower that the humans had built [Gen. 11:5]," or when "God shut Noah in the ark [Gen. 7:16]," you should not think that the unbegotten God himself went down or went up from some place. For the Father and Lord of all things, who is indescribable, does not come to some place, or walk about, or sleep, or get up, but remains in his own space, wherever that is, seeing sharply and hearing acutely without eyes or ears but by an indescribable power. He observes all things and knows all things; no one escapes his notice. He is not moved and he is not contained in a place, even in the whole world. He existed before ever the world came into existence. How, then, would he speak to someone, or be seen by someone, or appear on the smallest portion of the earth, when the people at Sinai could not even look at the glory of Moses, whom he sent.
>
> Justin Martyr, *Dialogue with Trypho the Jew* 127

the eyes of the contemporary philosophies, and that when he attempted to expound this faith to the non-Christian world he would do so, as far as possible, in terms of those philosophies.

Justin insists in his *Dialogue with Trypho the Jew* that he believes in only one God, and that this God is identical with the God of the Jews revealed in the Old Testament. In spite of this insistence on the unanimity between Christians and Jews in their belief in the God of the Old Testament, Justin's concept of God differed considerably from the Old Testament view of God. Justin thought of God as the transcendent, hidden God of the Middle Platonists. Such a God cannot interact directly with the created world. The God of the Old Testament, however, is frequently described as intervening directly in human affairs. He creates the heavens, the earth, and everything on the earth. The creation is described as God's direct action.[4] God converses directly with Noah, Abraham, Moses, Joshua, and others.[5] Various notable Old Testament personalities such as

4. Gen. 1–2.
5. See Gen. 6; 7; 12; 17; Exod. 3; 4; Lev. 1; Josh. 1; Isa. 6; Hosea 1.

Abraham, Moses, and Isaiah are said to have seen God or had a direct visitation from God.[6] The God Justin describes, however, does none of these things. He is above the whole created order and can interact with it only through an intermediary or go-between who can relate God to the creation. Justin's understanding of God depends conceptually on Middle Platonism, not on the Jewish Old Testament.

Justin understood the *Logos* to be the intermediary who made it possible for God to interact with and communicate with the created world. Trypho, a Jew, challenges Justin to show that Old Testament Scripture recognizes another God besides the creator of the universe. Justin responds by pointing to the passages in the Old Testament called theophanies, where God or an angel of God is said to appear to someone. He argues that the being who appeared in these theophanies was not the creator of the universe but another God distinct from the creator as a numerically separate being but united in his will as one with the creator. What Justin means is that the *Logos* is a second, distinct God, but the *Logos* never does anything that the creator does not want done.[7]

Justin argues that in the beginning God produced the *Logos* from himself. He is variously referred to in the Old Testament Scriptures as "the Glory of the Lord," "the Son," "Wisdom," "Angel," "God," "Lord," "*Logos*," or "Captain." The *Logos* was produced by an act of the Father's will. This act did not diminish or change the Father, any more than speaking a word diminishes us or lighting a second fire from a first diminishes the first fire in any way. Remember that *logos* often means "word," and that the Stoic philosophers had spoken of both an internal *logos*, meaning reason, and an external *logos*, meaning the reasoned expression of thoughts in words.[8] Theophilus, another Christian apologist of the second century, actually uses the technical terms the Stoics used and speaks of the *Logos* first being *internal* in God's mind; then, before God created anything, he produced the *Logos*

6. Gen. 18:1; Exod. 33:17–23; Isa. 6:1.
7. See Justin, *Dialogue with Trypho the Jew* 55–62.
8. See Justin, *Dialogue with Trypho the Jew* 61.

Theophilus on the *Logos*

Before anything was made, God had the *Logos* as his counselor, who was his mind and thought. But when God wished to make the things he had willed, he produced this *Logos* externally, "the firstborn of all creation." He himself was not emptied of *Logos*, but he produced the *Logos* and always associates with his *Logos*. This is what the Holy Scriptures and all the inspired writers teach us. One of the latter, named John, says, "In the beginning was the *Logos*, and the *Logos* was with God." This shows that at first there was only God, and the *Logos* was in him. Then he says, "And the *Logos* was God; all things were made through him, and not one thing was made without him." Therefore, since the *Logos* is God and has come forth from God, whenever the Father of the universe wills, he sends the *Logos* to some place where, being present, he is both heard and seen.

Theophilus, *To Autolycus* 2.22

---

externally from within himself. Tertullian, an apologist writing in the Latin language at the end of the second century and early in the third, suggests that the time the *Logos* became a separate being, distinct from God the Father, is indicated in Genesis 1:3 where God, for the first time in Scripture, is said to speak. Prior to this God was alone, Tertullian argues, yet not really alone, for he had his reason, which the Greeks called *logos*.[9]

The apologists considered the *Logos* to have served a twofold purpose in God's plan. First, he was the agent through whom the transcendent God created the material universe. They were in agreement with the statements made about the *Logos* in the opening verses of John's Gospel. There it is said that all things were made through the *Logos*, who was with God from the beginning and was God. In the thought of the apologists, the primary purpose of the *Logos* receiving a separate existence was to perform the work of creation. The transcendent God of the Middle Platonists could not directly involve himself in the creation of material things. He could only act on material things through an intermediary. The apologists were children of their time when they used the philosophical concept of the *Logos* to

---

9. Tertullian, *Against Praxeas* 5, 7.

> ### Tertullian on the Origin of the *Logos* as a Separate Being
>
> Prior to the creation of the world, before he had brought the Son into existence, . . . God was alone. He himself was the world, and space, and all things, but he was alone because there was no other being external to himself. But he was not quite alone at that time because he had his reason within himself, for God is rational. . . . This reason is his thought, which the Greeks call *logos* and we designate with the term "word."
>
> For as God had not yet dispatched his word, accordingly he had him with himself . . . as he silently pondered and determined what he would afterwards say by means of his word. . . .
>
> It was when God said, "Let there be light," that the Word took on his own appearance and attire, his own sound and voice. This going forth from God is the perfect birth of the Word. God first formed him to plan all things . . . then gave him birth to produce them.
>
> Tertullian, *Against Praxeas* 5, 7

explain how God produced the created order by means of his *Logos*. The other purpose the *Logos* served in the works of the apologists was as the agent of revelation. As we have already seen, it was the *Logos* whom the apologists thought visited and spoke to various people in the Old Testament. God himself did not speak with humans or appear to them.[10] This aspect of the work of the *Logos* reached its climax in the incarnation, when the *Logos* took flesh in the Virgin, was born, and lived among us.[11] For the apologists, the *Logos* was the medium between the transcendent God and the material universe. He was given existence for the purpose of creation and revelation.

The *Logos*, as God's reason in this way of thinking, had clearly existed with God eternally. God had never been without his reason. It could also be said that the *Logos* was God, for, as God's reason, he was a part of God and, even after he had been brought forth in a separate existence, he did not cease being God. These were positive points for *Logos* theology as Christians in

---

10. See Justin, *Dialogue with Trypho the Jew* 60.
11. See, for example, Justin, *Dialogue with Trypho the Jew* 63.

the second century began wrestling with the problem of how to think about the relationship between God the Father and the Son. As we saw in the preceding chapter, from the beginning Christians considered themselves to worship only one God, the same God who is revealed in the Jewish Scriptures, which Christians call the Old Testament. Christians also believed that Jesus was the Son of this one God and, therefore, God as well. But this seemed to some, both Christians and non-Christians, to leave them with two divine beings instead of one. The *Logos* theology provided a way for a group of philosophically educated Christians to explain how there could be an apparent diversity in the unity of God.

There were, however, some serious negative points in the *Logos* theology. One was that there seemed to be no way around the fact that this theology made it sound as though there is a first and a second God—in other words, two Gods. Another problem was that in this theology the *Logos* is not equal to God. He is subordinate to God the Father. Justin refers to him as "under" the creator in the sense of a servant.[12] He exists to serve God as mediator to the creation. His very existence seems to depend on the needs of creation. An even more serious defect in this theology is that the whole approach is based more on the philosophy of the Middle Platonists than on the Scriptures. As noted earlier, the view of God as transcendent and distant from the creation depends on Platonism and not on the description of God in the Old Testament. If the Middle Platonist view of God is not correct, then the role of the Son as mediator, as the apologists conceived it, must also be modified. The *Logos* theology as presented by the apologists of the second century was never considered heretical by the church at large, but it was considered inadequate for understanding the relationship between the Father and the Son. Later Christian thinkers such as Origen modified it significantly but continued to use it in some ways. Others rejected it completely and took totally different

12. See Justin, *Dialogue with Trypho the Jew* 56.4.

approaches to understanding the relationship between God the Father and the Son. We will consider some other approaches to the problem in the following chapters.

Points for Discussion

1. What was there about the Greek term *logos* that made it attractive to some Christians as a way to understand the relationship between God the Father and the Son?
2. Does the *Logos* theology seem to you to be a good way to understand the relationship of the Son to God? Why or why not?
3. What was there about the descriptions of God and his activities in the Old Testament that was problematic for anyone who thought of God from a Platonic perspective?
4. Is there anything in the Nicene Creed (see the creed in ch. 3) that reflects traces of the *Logos* theology? If so, what?

Resources for Further Reading

Daniélou, Jean. *Gospel Message and Hellenistic Culture*. Translated by J. A. Baker. Philadelphia: Westminster, 1973. See especially 345–57.

Justin Martyr. *Dialogue with Trypho the Jew*. In *ANF*, vol. 1. See 194–270. Also available at http://www.ccel.org/ccel/schaff/anf01.viii.iv.html.

Kelly, J. N. D. *Early Christian Doctrines*. 2nd ed. New York: Harper & Row, 1960. See especially 95–101.

Tertullian. *Against Praxeas*. In *ANF*, vol. 3. See 597–627. Also available at http://www.ccel.org/ccel/schaff/anf03.v.ix.html.

5

"He Who Has Seen Me Has Seen the Father"

The Monarchian Approach to God

Philip said to him, "Lord, show us the Father. . . ." Jesus replied to him, . . . "He who has seen me has seen the Father. What do you mean, 'Show us the Father'?"

John 14:8–9

Identifying the Major Personalities

Noetus of Smyrna: Considered to have introduced the teaching that there is no distinction between the Father and the Son.

Sabellius: Held the same views as Noetus about the Father and the Son, but was a more influential teacher.

Hippolytus: Third-century church father at Rome who wrote against Noetus and is a major source of our knowledge of Noetus's teachings.

Praxeas: Held similar views to Noetus. Tertullian addressed a treatise against him.

Theodotus: Considered to have introduced the doctrine that Jesus was not of divine origin but was a human adopted by God and given special power for his mission.

Paul of Samosata: A more influential teacher of the doctrine taught by Theodotus.

The word "monarchy" comes from two Greek words that together mean "rule by a single person." It was used politically for the rule of a king or a monarch. It was used in Christian doctrine to indicate the sole sovereignty of God. The term appears first in Christian literature in Tertullian's treatise *Against Praxeas*. Tertullian claims that a group of Christians who were concerned that they not be thought to worship two Gods used this term to describe their view of God. He called them monarchians. Modern church historians use the term to describe two different groups in the early church whose views, while similar in their general concern, were radically different from one another in their details. The common concern was to define the Christian doctrine of God in a way that would not appear to acknowledge two Gods. This, as was noted in chapter 4, was a major criticism of the *Logos* theology. The *Logos* appeared to be a second God. In the teaching of both groups of monarchians it is clear that there is only one God. The approaches they take to proving this, however, diverge radically from one another. Consequently, modern scholars add a qualifying word to the term "monarchian" to distinguish the two approaches. One is called dynamic monarchianism, and the other modalistic monarchianism. We will treat both approaches in this chapter, but we begin with the modalistic monarchians, the group to whom Tertullian applied the term "monarchian."

Modalistic Monarchianism

The modalistic monarchians identified Jesus of Nazareth completely with God the Father. It was generally accepted among Christians in the second century that Jesus was to be thought of as God, or divine. Most, however, like the unknown author of

2 Clement writing in the middle of the second century, did not think of this as a full identity with the Father. They thought, in other words, that the Father and the Son were two separate beings. They attributed the work of salvation to the Son and his death on the cross. The monarchians, on the other hand, said "Jesus *is* God." They emphasized the full divinity of Jesus and taught his complete identification with God the Father. They considered Jesus to be God the Father on earth. He was God in a human body. Father and Son were thought to be different modes in which the same God appeared at different times, or for different tasks. It would be similar to saying that the same man is a son in relation to his parents, a husband in relation to his wife, and a father in relation to his children. He may act differently in each situation, but he is the same person. And whatever happens to him in any one of these relationships happens to the one person.

This way of thinking of God and of Jesus presented a serious problem that was quickly recognized by many Christians. Total identification of Jesus with God meant that everything that happened to Jesus happened to God. There are many areas where we might think of problems if we understand Jesus to be the Father in flesh. To whom, for example, did Jesus pray when he is said to pray in the Gospels? Or was the God who created the universe a fetus in a woman's womb for nine months? What most Christians in the second and third centuries, however,

---

2 Clement on the Divine Identity of Jesus

Brothers and sisters, we must think of Jesus Christ in the way that we think of God, even as we think of the judge of the living and the dead. We must not think insignificant thoughts about our salvation. For when we think insignificant thoughts about him we also hope to receive insignificant things, and those who hear, as if we speak of insignificant things, sin, and we sin if we do not know from what we were called, and by whom, and to what place, and how many things Jesus Christ suffered on our behalf.

2 Clement 1.1

Noetus on the Identity of the Son with the Father

[Noetus] said that Christ himself is the Father, and that the Father himself was born, suffered, and died.

[The followers of Noetus] claim to demonstrate that there is one God . . . by saying, "If, then, I confess Christ to be God, then he is the Father, if indeed he is God. And Christ himself, being God, suffered. Therefore, the Father suffered, for he was the Father."

They use other testimonies and say, Thus it is written, "This is our God; another will not be reckoned with him. He discovered all knowledge and gave it to Jacob his servant and to Israel whom he loved. Later he appeared on earth and lived among humans" [Bar. 3:36–38]. You see, then, he says, This is God, who is alone, and was later seen and lived among humans. And in another passage it says, "Egypt has labored, and the business of the Ethiopians, and the tall Sabean men will come to you and be your slaves . . . and they will worship among you because God is in you, and they will pray among you because there is no God but you. For you are God and we did not know, O God of Israel, the Savior" [Isa. 45:14–15]. You see, he says, how the Scriptures proclaim one God, namely this one who appeared. These testimonies compel me, he says, since I confess one God, to submit him to suffering. For Christ was God, and being the Father himself he also suffered for us so that he could save us.

Hippolytus of Rome, *Contra Noetum* 1.2; 2.3, 5–7; ed. and trans. R. Butterworth (London: Heythrop Monographs, 1977), 43, 45, 47

---

found problematic in the assertion that Jesus was God in the flesh was that total identification of God the Father with Jesus meant that God the Father suffered and died on the cross. They gave those who held this view the name "patripassianists," which comes from two Greek words meaning "the Father suffered."

The discussion between the monarchians and their opponents—who also believed that the deity was one but was expressed in two separate beings, namely Father *and* Son—drew especially on the Gospel of John. The opponents to the monarchians cited John 1:18, "No one has ever seen God; the only-begotten Son who is in the Father's bosom has made him known." They argued that it was this Son, not the Father himself, who appeared on earth and made the Father known to humans. In John 20:17 Jesus says, "I am going to my Father and your Father, to my God and your God." If Noetus is correct, the opponents argued, to what Father is Jesus going, if he himself is the Father? In John 14:9 Jesus replies to Philip's request that he show them the Father by saying, "He who has seen me has seen the Father." The monarchians used this verse as proof of their doctrine that Jesus was the Father. Their opponents replied that Jesus was the image of the Father and that what he means is that if you have seen me, you have seen what the Father is like because I am his image.[1] Tertullian indicates that John 10:30 was a favorite verse of the monarchians. There Jesus says, "I and my Father are one." What they fail to notice, Tertullian says, is that *two persons* are mentioned, "I and my Father," and that the verb "are" is plural, which would be incorrect if the subject were singular. Furthermore, he adds, Jesus does not say we are one *person*, but one *thing*, for he uses the neuter form of the word "one." This shows, he argues, that what Jesus is speaking of is not a single person, but "unity, likeness, conjunction, love on the part of the Father who loves the Son, and obedience on the part of the Son who obeys the Father's will." "When Jesus says 'I and the Father [we] are one,' he shows that they are two whom he makes equal and joins together."[2]

Somewhat later the doctrine of Noetus was taken up by a man named Sabellius. He is the most famous proponent of the teaching we call modalistic monarchianism. In fact, modalistic monarchianism was later called Sabellianism after Sabellius. We first hear of him from Hippolytus of Rome, who says that Sabellius was in Rome during the time when Zephyrinus was bishop there—that is, between AD 199 and 222. Sabellius was like Noetus in identifying the Son with God the Father and holding the patripassianist view that when the Son suffered and died, it was the Father who suffered and died. He took the additional step of introducing the Holy Spirit into the equation, so that when the Son was no longer on earth the Father continued to

---

1. See Hippolytus of Rome, *Contra Noetum* 5–7.
2. Tertullian, *Against Praxeas* 22. See also Hippolytus of Rome, *Contra Noetum* 7.

> ### Sabellius on the Identity of the Son and the Spirit with the Father
>
> [Sabellius] teaches . . . that the Father, the Son, and the Spirit are the same, so that one substance has three names. Just as a human being has a body, soul, and spirit, the Father is the body, so to speak, the Son is the soul, and the Holy Spirit is to the deity what the spirit is to a human being. Or, to use another analogy, it is like the sun, which consists of one substance but has three activities—illumination, heat, and the spherical shape itself. The Spirit is the warm, seething heat, the Son is the illumination, and the Father is the form itself of the whole substance. Now the Son was once sent forth like a sunray, and when he had accomplished in the world everything related to the plan of the gospel and human salvation, he was again taken up into heaven, like a sunray that is sent forth and again returns into the sun. And the Holy Spirit was sent into the world both once for all and at particular times on individuals considered worthy of this. Such people are revitalized and stimulated by the warmth and heat, so to speak, which comes from the power and fellowship of the Spirit. This is what they teach.
>
> Epiphanius, *Panarion* 62.1.4–9

be present in the mode of the Holy Spirit. Noetus seems not to have considered the Holy Spirit in his teaching but to have focused solely on the Son and his relationship to the Father.

Sabellius identified the Father with the divine substance and taught that the Son and the Spirit were individual manifestations of that substance for particular tasks, such as the saving of humanity from sin or the inspiring of special people. An unknown Christian writing under the name of Athanasius in the fourth century says that Sabellius "was out of his mind when he said that the Father is Son and the Son Father, one in substance but two in name." He says that Sabellius used the Pauline statement about the Holy Spirit in 1 Corinthians 12:4 to argue that "just as 'there is a diversity of gifts but the same Spirit,' so too the Father is the same, but he is expanded into Son and Spirit." "This is absurd," he argues, "for if it is the same with God as it is with the Spirit, the Father will be *Logos* and Holy Spirit, becoming Father to one, *Logos* to another, and Spirit to yet another, accommodating himself to the need of each person." This means, he continues, that "while he is Son in name, or Spirit in name, in truth he is always the Father alone." Furthermore, he says, if the Son "became human in name but in truth did not visit us, then he lied when he said, 'I and the Father,' because in reality he was the Father."[3]

What does it mean to call Jesus God? The doctrine of Noetus and Sabellius represents one of the answers given to this question in the second and early third centuries. It means to identify Jesus with God the Father. This honors Jesus by attributing full divinity to him. It has the negative effect, however, of dishonoring the Father, for it also means that God the Father must be identified completely with the human Jesus, and whatever happened to him must be assumed to have happened to God the Father. It raises problems concerning his birth and such things as Jesus's prayers in the Gospels and statements he makes about the relationship between himself and the Father. The most problematic aspect of this identification, however, is that it means one must assert that God the Father died on the cross. Most people found it impossible to think that the God and Father of the universe was nailed to a cross, died, and lay three days as a corpse in a tomb. It was for this reason that this view of Jesus was considered unacceptable by the larger church.

Dynamic Monarchianism

Another answer given to the question of the relation between Jesus and God in the second- and third-century church is called dynamic monarchianism. This descriptive title was coined by modern scholars to distinguish this group of monarchians from those called modalistic monarchians. Those Christians who held the view called dynamic monarchianism believed that Jesus was an ordinary man adopted for a special mission by God at his baptism. They understood the descent of the Spirit described

3. See Pseudo-Athanasius, Oration 4, *Against the Arians* 25.

Theodotus on Jesus as a Man with a Divine Gift

[Theodotus taught that it was] because Jesus had become very religious that the Christ descended on him from above in the form of a dove when he was baptized in the Jordan. This is why Jesus did not do mighty works before the descent and manifestation of the Spirit in him. It is the Spirit who designates him the Christ. [The followers of Theodotus] do not think Jesus became God even at the time of the descent of the Spirit. Others, however, think he did after the resurrection from the dead.

Hippolytus, *Refutation of All Heresies* 7.35

---

in the accounts of Jesus's baptism in the Gospels to indicate the coming of a special *power* of God upon Jesus of Nazareth. *Dynamis* is a Greek word that means "power"; hence modern scholars call this view *dynamic* monarchianism.

The person attributed with originating this teaching was said to be a cobbler from Constantinople named Theodotus. He went to Rome about AD 190. Hippolytus, who is an early source of our knowledge of what Theodotus taught, says that he held correct views about God as creator. He taught that Jesus, however, was a mere man, like all other human beings, except that he had been born of a virgin after the Holy Spirit had overshadowed his mother Mary. This latter is an allusion, of course, to the story of the annunciation in Luke 1:35. Jesus did not possess divine power until the Holy Spirit descended on him at his baptism in the Jordan. The dynamic monarchians avoided the error of teaching that there were two Gods by claiming that Jesus was not God but a human being whom God filled with his Spirit in a unique way. They disagreed on whether he ever became God, but they were in complete agreement that he was not God before he was filled with the power or Spirit of God at his baptism.

The Theodotians argued that their view of Jesus had been held by all earlier Christians, including the apostles, and that this view had been altered only when Zephyrinus was bishop of Rome (AD 199–217). This statement concerning the apostles and the earliest Christians was made in reference to certain statements about Jesus in the Bible. Theodotus is said to have used John 8:40, for example, in which Jesus says, "But now you seek to kill me, a man who has told you the truth," to show that Jesus himself claimed to be a man. Deuteronomy 18:15, "The Lord will raise up a prophet like me for you from your brothers," was also used to argue that Jesus was only a man. Most Christians understood Deuteronomy 18:15 to be a statement Moses made about the Christ who was to come. Because Moses was a man, the Theodotians argued, and he said that the anticipated prophet would be like him and from among their brothers, the Christ was also a man. Isaiah 53 was another passage in the Old Testament that most Christians thought spoke of the suffering of the Christ. But the Theodotians pointed out that Isaiah 53:3–4 speaks of a *man* who is weak, beaten, and dishonored. They also noted that in 1 Timothy 2:5 Paul says that the mediator "between God and men" is "the *man* Christ Jesus." The Theodotians seem to have had a special liking for Acts 2:22, where they said that the apostles identified Jesus as "a man attested to you by God by means of powerful deeds."[4]

Epiphanius, a fourth-century defender of orthodoxy, asserted that Theodotus invented this doctrine because he had denied Christ in a persecution, and that when Christians later questioned him about it, he defended himself by saying that he had not denied God, only a man. After this he developed his doctrine that Christ was only a man. This, however, is only a story Epiphanius had heard. It is not known if it is true or not.[5]

Paul of Samosata was the most significant and notorious dynamic monarchian. He was bishop of Antioch of Syria in the mid-third century. He was removed from his position by a synod of bishops who met in Antioch in AD 268. He taught that Jesus was a normal man born as all men are born. He was not

4. See Epiphanius, *Panarion* 54, for the passages of Scripture used by Theodotus and his followers.
5. Epiphanius, *Panarion* 54.3–7. The same story is told in Filastrius, *Book of Various Heresies* 22.

born of a virgin and he did not descend to earth from above. Christ did not exist before his existence on earth. It appears that Paul refused to allow Christ to be worshiped in the church where he was bishop. Eusebius, who wrote in the fourth century, says that Paul would not allow psalms addressed to Christ to be sung in the church.[6] This would have been in harmony with Paul's view that Jesus was not of divine origin. He is supposed to have said, "Jesus Christ is from below," meaning that he was from the earth like all humans and not from heaven.[7]

Both monarchian positions were objections to the *Logos* theology begun by the second-century apologists. Both positions were rejected by the larger church. The modalistic monarchian position was rejected primarily because it involved God the Father in suffering and death, and the dynamic monarchian position was rejected because it treated the Son as an ordinary man who was filled with the divine Spirit and given power for a divine mission. The two monarchian positions were alike in denying the preexistence of the Son from all eternity with the Father. The *Logos* theology considered in chapter 4, on the other hand, asserted the eternal existence of the *Logos* with God the Father. This position was rejected, however, because it made the *Logos* a second God subordinate to God the Father. A generally acceptable answer to the question "What does it mean to call Jesus God?" had not yet been found in the first part of the third century.

Points for Discussion

1. What was the pressing concern of those early Christians referred to as monarchians?
2. Explain the difference between modalistic monarchians and dynamic monarchians.

6. Eusebius, *Ecclesiastical History* 7.30.10–11.
7. Eusebius, *Ecclesiastical History* 7.30.11.

3. What was the major objection to the modalistic monarchian position by some Christians?
4. What was the major objection to the dynamic monarchian position by most Christians?
5. Do either of the monarchian positions appeal to you? Why?

Resources for Further Reading

Heine, Ronald E. "Articulating Identity." In *The Cambridge History of Early Christian Literature*, edited by Frances Young, Lewis Ayres, and Andrew Louth, 200–221. Cambridge: Cambridge University Press, 2004. See especially 200–206.

Hippolytus. *Refutation of All Heresies*. In *ANF*, vol. 5. See especially book 7, ch. 23 (Theodotus); book 9, ch. 3; and book 10, ch. 23 (Noetus). Also available at http://www.ccel.org/fathers.html.

Tertullian. *Against Praxeas*. In *ANF*, vol. 3. Also available at http://www.ccel.org/ccel/schaff/anf03.v.ix.i.html.

6

"Today I Have Begotten You"

Origen and the Eternal Generation of the Son

> The Lord said to me, "You are my son; today
> I have begotten you."
>
> Psalm 2:7

Identifying the Major Personalities

Origen: A Christian teacher in Alexandria, Egypt, and later in Caesarea, Palestine, who taught and wrote in the first half of the third century. He was the most influential Greek-speaking teacher in the ancient church. He wrote commentaries on most books of the Bible, produced a massive work comparing texts of the Greek translation of the Old Testament with the Hebrew text, preached homilies on most of the Old Testament and some of the New, wrote a major defense of Christianity against a philosopher, and composed what is usually considered the first systematic study of Christian theology.

The question of the relationship of the Son to the Father occupied the mind of the early Christians from at least the mid-second century through the first quarter of the fourth, as we will see in the next chapter. Two questions in particular troubled the early Christian mind. If the Son is divine—that is, God—do Christians not, then, recognize and worship two Gods? And if the second divine being is referred to as the (only) begotten Son of God, does that not imply a beginning for the Son? The *Logos* theologians[1] answered the second question by appealing to the term *logos*, which means, among other things, "reason." They could point to John 1:1–2, where this terminology is used, and argue that God has never been without *logos*. God later gave separate existence to the *Logos* for the purpose of creating the world. The prologue to John's Gospel identifies the *Logos* as the divine that became incarnate later in Jesus. These Christian thinkers answered the question of the eternity of the Son by appealing to the abstract philosophical concept of *logos*. But, as we have seen, there were several objections to this philosophical approach to understanding the deity. Others sidestepped the second question by answering the first with the simple assertion that the being known as Jesus Christ in the New Testament was God the Father himself operating in a different mode from that in which he had created the universe and given the law. Still others simplified the answer in the other direction by arguing that Jesus was not divine but a normal mortal man whom God chose and provided with a special power for a particular task. Origen was aware of these attempts to answer the question concerning the Son's relationship to the Father and argued with them in several places, usually without mentioning explicitly that he was doing so. He was certainly influenced by the *Logos* theology, but he was also severely critical of it at certain points.

The Eternal Existence of the Son

The key concept that Origen used to understand and explain Jesus Christ and his relationship to God was that of Son. He argued that the Son had existed from all eternity with God. This teaching is referred to as the eternal generation or begetting of the

1. See ch. 4.

An Example from Porphyry of Terms Whose Meanings Depend on One Another

Whenever things introduce or eliminate each other they are simultaneous. . . . For instance, a father is a father when taken together with his son, for it is together with his son that he possesses the being of a father, and a person comes to be a father when he comes to have a son. So "father" introduces "son" along with itself, and "son" introduces "father" along with itself. Conversely, without a son there cannot be a father. . . . Therefore, since "father" and "son" introduce each other, and when one is eliminated the other is as well, these will be simultaneous by nature.

> Porphyry, *On Aristotle's Categories*, trans. S. K. Strange (London: Duckworth, 1992), 123 (translation modified)

Son. Origen did not, however, use the *Logos* concept, as the *Logos* theologians had done, to prove this. He provided two arguments, one drawn from philosophy and the other from Scripture. The two arguments are often interwoven in Origen's discussions, but we will treat them separately, so far as that is possible.

We begin with the philosophical argument for the eternal existence of the Son alongside the Father. Origen had a philosophical education. The study of philosophy at that time and for several succeeding centuries began with the reading of Aristotle's *Categories*. Origen would have been familiar with the arguments in this book, in which Aristotle sets out what he considers to be the various categories one can apply in defining a term, or the reality to which the term points. For example, if a man stands before us, we can ask, what is it? This would fall under Aristotle's category of substance. The answer would be a male human being. Or we could apply the category of quality and ask, what are its qualities? An answer might be an educated male who speaks English. One of Aristotle's categories for definition is what he calls "relation." This category demands a reference to another object of comparison or relation. Certain terms are relational by definition. Aristotle calls these terms "correlatives." Such terms both support and eliminate one another. If one term

Origen on the Eternity of the Son

The first thing we must know is that there is a divine nature in Christ, because he is the only-begotten Son of the Father, and a human nature that he took up only recently for the sake of the economy of salvation. First, we must discover what the only-begotten Son of God is. . . . Solomon called him Wisdom, when he said, as Wisdom speaking, "The Lord created me as the beginning of his ways for his works. I was founded before he made anything, including the ages. He begot me in the beginning before he made the earth, before the fountains of waters came forth, before the mountains and all the hills were made firm" [Prov. 8:22–25]. . . . No one, however, should think that we mean something abstract without substance when we call him the "Wisdom of God." . . . How can anyone think or believe that there was ever a time, even the shortest moment, when God the Father existed without the begetting of this Wisdom? . . . [W]e know that God was always Father of his only-begotten Son, who was born from him and receives what he is from him, but without any beginning. . . . John . . . defines the Word to be God when he says, "And the Word was God, and he was in the beginning with God" [John 1:1–2]. But let the person who posits a beginning for God's Word or his Wisdom beware that he not rather defame the unbegotten Father himself when he denies that he was always Father and, in all previous times or ages, had begotten the Word and possessed Wisdom.

Origen, *On First Principles* 1.2.1–3

is removed, so is the other. So, if we say of our example man, in answer to the relation question, he is a husband, this identification demands that there is also a wife. Remove the term "wife," and there can be no husband. Aristotle illustrates his argument with the terms "master" and "slave." If there is no master, there can be no slave, and vice versa.[2]

Origen probably did not take his argument directly from Aristotle. Aristotle's *Categories*, as noted above, formed the basis of philosophical education in Origen's time. The Platonic schools, with whose views Origen was in sympathy, began by discussing the *Categories*. One of the important points they discussed was the fact that terms considered relatives are simultaneous by nature—that is, they must exist at the same time. Porphyry,

2. See Aristotle, *Categories* 7b15ff.

Origen on John 1:1

[John] wrote in a very straightforward manner . . . , "In the beginning was the *Logos.*" He chooses his words carefully. The word "became" refers to the flesh [John 1:14]; the word "was" refers to his divinity [John 1:1]. It would have been more appropriate to use "is" of the *Logos* of God, but because he was showing the existence of the *Logos* as distinct from the incarnation, which occurred at a particular time, the evangelist used "was" instead of "is."

But we must not understand words to have their ordinary meanings when they are used of eternal things. Sometimes these words indicate a temporally limited existence. For example, "was" indicates something that once existed but no longer is; likewise, "is" points to what is now in existence, just as "will be" indicates what will exist. But since the *Logos* of God is eternal, being God, we must not take words used of him in a temporal sense, because he is not subject to time. It is possible, nevertheless, to search out their meaning from the expressions themselves the theologian uses. For at the very beginning of his treatise, he writes, "In the beginning was the *Logos.*" . . . John did not say, "The *Logos* came to be in the beginning," or "the *Logos* was made in the beginning," but "In the beginning was the *Logos.*" For he was in the beginning when he made the heaven and the earth. For if "all things were made by him," and heaven and earth are a part of the "all things," he himself was the creator responsible for bringing them into being.

Origen, *Commentary on John*, fragment 2

---

a Platonist philosopher who claimed to have met Origen when he was a young man, wrote a commentary on Aristotle's *Categories*. He uses the "father-son" relationship to illustrate the simultaneous nature of relatives. There can only be a father, Porphyry argues, when there is a son. Eliminate the concept of son and you simultaneously eliminate that of father.

Origen uses the same illustrations that the philosophers used in their discussion of relative relationships to argue that if God has always existed as Father, then he must also have always had the Son. "Just as no one can be a father," he says, "if there is no son, neither can anyone be a master without a possession or a slave."[3] This constitutes the philosophical basis of Origen's

---

3. Origen, *On First Principles* 1.2.10.

argument for the eternal existence of the Son with the Father. If one assumes that the title Father is appropriate for God at all times, and most early Christians would have agreed that it was, then it is necessary to assume also that the Son has always existed with the Father.

There were various exegetical arguments that Origen used to prove the eternity of the Son. We will look at only two. The first is the language used of the *Logos* in John 1:1. There the evangelist says, "In the beginning *was* the *Logos* [Word], and the *Logos was* with God, and the *Logos was* God." Origen contrasts the meaning of the verb "was" with the meaning of the verb "came to be" and argues that this distinction in meaning points to the Gospel of John teaching the eternal existence of the *Logos*/Son with God. To show the difference in meaning, I will translate John 1:1 again, but I will substitute the verb "came to be" for the verb "was" in the statement. "In the beginning the *Logos* [Word] *came to be*, and the *Logos came to be* with God, and the *Logos came to be* God." When we make this substitution it is easy to see the point of Origen's argument. If John had used the verb "came to be," he would have indicated that the *Logos* had not existed *before* the beginning. To *come to be* indicates that there is a beginning point. To *be,* on the other hand, suggests nothing about origination. Origen thinks that John chose this particular verb very intentionally to make a statement about the *Logos*. He points out that the verb "came to be" occurs in a few statements made in some of the prophetic writings of the Old Testament in clauses structured like the clause in John 1:1, which says, "And the *Logos* was with God." He cites Hosea 1:1, where it says "The *Logos* [Word] of the Lord . . . came to be with Hosea."[4] This, Origen argues, is how Scripture describes the divine visitation to human beings. The *Logos* visits Hosea with a message for him to deliver to the people of God. The *Logos* has not been with Hosea eternally; there was a point

---

4. Translated from the Septuagint, the Greek translation of the Bible that Origen used.

in time when Hosea received a divine visitation. On the other hand, Origen says, the *Logos* "does not *come to be* 'with God' as though previously he were not with him, but because he is always with the Father, it is said, 'And the *Logos was* with God,' for he did not *come to be* with God." The use of the verb "was" instead of "came to be" in John 1:1 allows Origen to conclude, "Before all time and eternity 'the Logos was in the beginning,' and the Logos was with God."[5]

Another exegetical argument Origen used to prove the eternal existence of the Son of God involved the interpretation of Psalm 2:7, "You are my son, today I have begotten you," especially as that verse had been used in Hebrews.[6] Origen argues that there is no such thing as time with God. He exists in an eternal present, without past or future. Therefore, when the psalmist says, "Today I have begotten you," he is referring to the timeless day in which God exists. Consequently, one cannot speak of a time when the Son was born. As Origen puts it, "Neither the beginning nor the day of his begetting is to be found."[7]

The Role of the Doctrine of the Eternal Existence of the Son

The importance of these arguments concerning the eternity of the Son was tied directly to the belief that the Son was divine, or God. God was believed to be without beginning or end. If the Son is also God, then the same must be true of him as well. Origen believed that there were two natures in Christ, a divine nature and a human nature, but the divine was certainly, for him, the more important. He noted, for example, that four Gospels are recognized by the church. He considered the Gospel of John, however, to be the most important of the Gospels

---

5. *Origen: Commentary on the Gospel according to John, Books 1–10*, trans. Ronald E. Heine, FOTC 80 (Washington, DC: The Catholic University of America Press, 1989), 96–97, translation modified.

6. See Heb. 1:5; 5:5–6; 7:3, 17.

7. *Origen: Commentary on John*, 74, translation modified.

Origen on One God, but Father and Son

[W]e worship but *one God*, the Father and the Son. . . . And we do not *worship to an extravagant degree a man who appeared recently* as though he did not exist previously. For we believe him who says, "Before Abraham was I am," and who affirms, "I am the truth." None of us is so stupid as to suppose that before the date of Christ's manifestation the truth did not exist. Therefore we worship the Father of the truth and the Son who is the truth; they are two distinct existences, but one in mental unity, in agreement, and in identity of will. Thus he who has seen the Son . . . has seen God in him who is God's image.

Origen, *Against Celsus* 8.12; in Origen, *Contra Celsum*, trans. H. Chadwick (Cambridge: Cambridge University Press, 1965), 460–61

---

because it presents the divinity of Christ more clearly than the others. He asserted that statements of Jesus found only in the Gospel of John, such as the following, show Jesus's divinity: "I am the light of the world," "I am the way, the truth, and the life," and so forth.[8]

The divinity of Christ, Origen thought, defines what Christ is in and of himself. The humanity was what he took on himself for our sakes. Humanity does not define what he is. He is God.[9] On the other hand, he is a being distinct from God. The "Son is other than the Father," Origen says. To prove this, and also to prove that the Son is coeternal with the Father, he repeats Aristotle's argument concerning relative terms: "[I]t is necessary that a son be the son of a father and that a father be the father of a son."[10] In the first book of his *Commentary on Matthew*, Origen reflects on the implications of Paul's statements in Philippians 2:5–8 about Christ being in the form of God, but emptying himself to become a human, even a slave, and to die on a cross. This statement, he asserts, shows "that his birth was not of the sort that one who did not previously exist began to be." It indicates, to the contrary that "one who previously existed and

---

8. *Origen: Commentary on John*, 37.
9. *Origen: Commentary on John*, 55–56.
10. *Origen: Commentary on John*, 309.

'was in the form of God' came in order . . . to take 'the form of a slave.'"[11] The preexistence of the Son in all eternity with God the Father was basic to Origen's understanding of Jesus Christ.

The *Logos* theologians had also stressed the eternal existence of the *Logos* with God. Origen clearly stood in their tradition, but he also differed from them, as the preceding discussions should make apparent. He has two major critiques of the *Logos* theology as it had been expressed by his predecessors. First, he argues at great length against those who thought that the expression *Logos* was the key to understanding the nature of Christ. *Logos*, he argues, is simply one among a long list of descriptive titles—such as the way, the truth, the life, the resurrection, the good shepherd, and so on—applied to Christ in the Bible. One must treat the title *Logos* in the same way one treats these other titles and investigate each one to see in what sense it is appropriate to use this particular concept of Christ. The title *Logos* has no inherent priority over any of the other titles. Each title communicates something important about Christ, but no single title is definitive of what Christ is, as the *Logos* theologians thought the title *Logos* was.[12]

Origen's second critique of the *Logos* theology was its focus on Psalm 45:1 as the explanation for the origin of the *Logos*. There the psalmist says in the Septuagint translation, "My heart has brought forth a good word [*logos*]." Some of the Christian apologists of the second century[13] had understood God to be the speaker of these words and identified the *logos* mentioned in Psalm 45:1 with the *Logos* mentioned in John 1:1. Psalm 45:1, they thought, spoke of the origin of the *Logos* and explained where the *Logos* was prior to his generation by God. Tertullian, who made this identification, even refers to the "womb" of God's

11. Origen's *Commentary on Matthew* has been lost. The quotation is preserved in a later *Apology for Origen* written in the fourth century: *St. Pamphilus: Apology for Origen*, trans. T. P. Scheck, FOTC 120 (Washington, DC: The Catholic University of America Press, 2010), 93–94.

12. *Origen: Commentary on John*, 59–91.

13. See ch. 4.

heart.[14] They explained the origin of the *Logos* on the analogy of someone uttering a spoken word. Origen objects strongly to this view. He argues that the speaker of these words must be David, not God. The *Logos* theologians also thought that this verse explained what the Son of God is. They seem to think, Origen says, that the Son is an expression of the Father occurring in syllables. He attacks this view with the theological argument that such a doctrine fails to give substance to the Son of God. A pronounced word has no substance. No one can understand a pronounced word to be a son. He suggests instead that "the good word" Psalm 45:1 refers to should be understood to be a prophecy about Christ uttered by David. Origen believed that the Son had existed eternally with God the Father, but as a Son and not as a word in the Father's heart.

Origen's view of Christ contributed significantly to what was to become the orthodox view accepted at Nicaea in the fourth century and passed on in the Nicene Creed. The bishops who met at Nicaea modified some of his views and suppressed others, but his thinking had a major impact on what came to be considered the correct way of understanding the nature of Christ.

Points for Discussion

1. In what ways was Origen's doctrine of the Son of God like that of the *Logos* theologians, and in what ways was it different?
2. How does Origen's doctrine of the Son of God differ from that of the modalistic monarchians?
3. Do you find Origen's arguments for the eternal begetting of the Son convincing? Why?
4. Do you think that the doctrine that the Son has always existed with the Father is important? Why?
5. Are there any parts of the Nicene Creed (see ch. 3) that reflect this doctrine?

14. Tertullian, *Against Praxeas* 7.1, as does Theophilus, *To Autolycus* 2.22.

Resources for Further Reading

Daniélou, Jean. *Gospel Message and Hellenistic Culture.* Translated by J. A. Baker. Philadelphia: Westminster, 1973. See especially 375–86.

Heine, Ronald E. *Origen: Scholarship in the Service of the Church.* Oxford: Oxford University Press, 2010. See especially 93–103, 139–40.

Origen. *Commentary on the Gospel according to John, Books 1–10.* Translated by Ronald E. Heine. FOTC 80. Washington, DC: The Catholic University of America Press, 1989. See especially Book 1.151–Book 2.69.

Origen. *On First Principles.* Translated by G. W. Butterworth. 1936. Reprint, Gloucester, MA: Peter Smith, 1973. See Book 1, ch. 2.

Older translations of the two works above can be found online in the *Ante-Nicene Fathers* series at http://www.ccel.org/fathers.html in volumes 4 and 9.

7

"One God the Father" and "One Lord Jesus Christ"

Arius and the Council of Nicaea

> But for us there is one God the Father . . . and one Lord Jesus Christ.
>
> 1 Corinthians 8:6

Identifying the Major Personalities

Arius: A presbyter/priest in Alexandria who taught that Christ was a created being.

Constantine: The first Christian emperor (AD 312–37) of the Roman Empire. He invited all the bishops in the world to a council at Nicaea in AD 325 to settle the theological debate Arius's teaching had initiated.

Alexander: Bishop of Alexandria who first objected to Arius's teaching.

Athanasius: Secretary to Alexander and his successor as bishop of Alexandria. A strong opponent of the teaching of Arius.

Eusebius: Influential bishop of Caesarea who opposed Arius, but not so strongly as Athanasius. Best known for his famous *Ecclesiastical History*, which is the first history of the church.

What does it mean to confess Jesus Christ to be God? We have looked at three different answers Christians gave to that question in the second and third centuries. Some thought of Christ as God's *Logos* or reason, as the prologue to John's Gospel speaks of him. This answer offered a ready explanation for the identity between the Father and the Son, the latter being identified with the *Logos*. God was never without reason or *Logos*, so the Son shared in God's eternity. When God desired to create, he brought forth the *Logos* by an act of his will as a being external to himself. The *Logos* then became the means by which God created all things, and later the means by which he communicated with and finally acted to save his creation. The *Logos* was clearly fully God. But it seemed to many that this made the *Logos* a second God of a lower rank than God the Father. Others in the late second century tried to answer the question of how the Son could be God without there being two Gods by arguing that the being who was seen as the Son and who lived among humans was, in fact, God the Father himself operating in the mode of Savior of humanity rather than in that of creator and sustainer of the universe. This was rejected because it necessitated assuming too many things to have happened to God that most people did not think could happen to deity. The other late second-century suggestion for resolving the problem of the two apparent Gods in the Christian faith asserted that Jesus was not God but merely a very religious man whom God chose for a special mission and endowed with an extraordinary power called the Christ that descended on him at his baptism. Many, however, found this answer inadequate because it did not honor Jesus sufficiently and it went contrary to many statements in the Scriptures that pointed to the deity of Jesus. We will look at two additional answers given to the question of the relationship of the Son to the Father in this chapter.

Arius and the Uniqueness of God

In the early fourth century a priest named Arius in Alexandria, Egypt, proposed another way of answering the question of the relationship between the Father and the Son. Arius believed that God is absolutely unique. No other being can share his qualities. The term that Arius chose to express this was "unbegotten." He considered this term to mean to be without beginning, or never to have come into existence, but to have existed eternally. There never was a time when God did not exist. No other being, Arius thought, shares this with God, not even the Son. The Father is unbegotten; the Son is begotten. To be begotten means to be produced by or born from another being. In human terms it means to be produced by or born of a father and mother. This term is used of the birth of Jesus in the Gospels, though the teaching of his birth from a virgin limits its use to his being born of Mary.[1] When John speaks of the Son's relationship to God the Father he calls him the "only-begotten" Son of God.[2] It was biblical to speak of the Son as a begotten being. The term "unbegotten," however, is not used of God in the Bible. All Christians would have agreed with Arius that God was without beginning. Most of them also believed, however, that the Son shared in this eternal nature of God and that there never was a time when the Son did not exist as well. Origen, for example, had argued that the Son was eternally begotten by the Father, so that there never was a time when the Father did not have the Son. Arius thought, on the other hand, that if any other being shared in what God is, which includes his nature of being without beginning, there would then be more than one God. So, he argued, because God is unique, everything else must have been created by God and have had a beginning.

The Son, therefore, Arius taught, had a beginning; only the Father is without beginning. "There was a time," Arius said, "when he [that is, the Son] did not exist; before he was brought into being, he did not exist." The Father's substance is different from that of the Son because he did not have a beginning. He was God even when the Son did not exist. Because Arius

1. See Matt. 1:16; 2:1; Luke 1:35; John 18:37.
2. John 1:14, 18.

Arius's Statement of Faith

We acknowledge one God who is alone unbegotten, alone eternal, alone without beginning, alone true, alone possessor of immortality, alone wise, alone good, alone ruler, judge, administrator, and manager of all things, without change or alteration, just and good. He is God of the law, the prophets, and the New Testament. He begot an only-begotten Son before eternal times "through whom also he has made the ages" [Heb. 1:2] and the universe. He begot him not in appearance, but in reality, and gave him existence by his own will, a perfect creature of God, without change or alteration, but not as one of the creatures; a begotten being, but not as one of the begotten beings . . . , created before times and ages, having received his life and existence from the Father. . . . God, who is the cause of all things, is uniquely alone without beginning. But the Son, who was begotten outside of time by the Father, and was created and established before the ages, did not exist before he was begotten, but when he had been begotten outside of time before all things, he alone was caused to exist by the Father. For he is not eternal, or coeternal with the Father, nor does he share in the Father's unbegotten nature.

As presented in Athanasius, *De Synodis* 16; PG 26:708D–709C

---

thought the Son's substance to be different from that of the Father, even though he sometimes used the word "begotten" to describe the origin of the Son, he could not have used the word with its normal meaning.

In normal usage, when a child is said to be begotten by a father or born of a mother, it means that the child shares in the human nature of her parents. She is human, just as her parents are human. But Arius did not mean that the Son is divine in the same way that God the Father is divine. The more accurate word that Arius used to describe the origin of the Son was the word "created." Arius considered the Son to be one of God's creations. The distinction between being begotten by God and created by God is that what is begotten shares in the substance or nature of the begetter. A child, for example, is begotten by a father. The child has the same substance as the father; that is, the child is a human being of flesh and blood as is the father. If the same father builds a house, the house is created by the father, but it is not human. It does not share in his substance. It is not what he is. This is what the church was arguing about when it debated whether the Son was begotten by God or created by God. What is created by God is not God. What is begotten is. God created Adam from the dust of the earth. Adam was not divine. This was the problem many Christians saw in Arius's teaching about the Son being created by God. It meant that the Son was not God.

When Arius talked about the Son being a created being, he did not mean that he was a human like other humans, or even an angel like other angels. When he spoke of the Son not existing before he was created, he was not referring to the human birth of Jesus from Mary, as recorded in the Gospels. Arius did not mean the human Jesus at all when he referred to the Son's origin. He thought the Son was the first of all created beings, made by God before anything else existed, and made to be the

---

Constantine's Concern at Nicaea according to a Fifth-Century Report

The excellent emperor . . . exhorted the bishops to unanimity and agreement; he reminded them of the cruelty of the late emperors, and of the . . . peace which God had granted them during his reign and by his efforts. He pointed out how dreadful it was . . . that at the very time when their enemies were destroyed and no one dared oppose them, they should attack one another . . . , especially since they were debating holy things for which they had the written teachings of the Holy Spirit. "For the Gospels," he said, "the apostolic writings, and the oracles of the ancient prophets, clearly teach us what we ought to believe about the divine nature. Let us, then, put aside all contentious arguments and seek the solution for the questions under discussion in the divinely inspired word." With these and similar exhortations he . . . addressed the bishops . . . laboring to bring about their unanimity in the apostolic doctrines. Most members of the synod were convinced by his arguments, established harmony among themselves, and embraced sound doctrine. There were, however, a few . . . who opposed these doctrines.

Theodoret, *The Ecclesiastical History* 1.6; *NPNF*, vol. 3 (2nd series), 92–93 (translation modified)

---

agent through whom God would create all things. But he was, nevertheless, not God, and he did not exist before his creation. Arius defended the uniqueness of God by denying that the Son was God. There is only one God; the Son was one of God's creations.

The Council of Nicaea

Had Arius lived a century earlier his teachings would probably not have caused the furor that they caused. Some would have accepted his views and others would have dismissed them. They would probably have been passed over eventually as the teachings of the monarchians and those of the *Logos* theologians were dismissed and passed over. But Arius put forth his views on the relationship between the Father and the Son when Constantine, the first Christian emperor of the Roman Empire, had just acquired possession of the eastern, Greek-speaking section of the empire. One of Constantine's first actions when he won control of the western portion of the empire a few years earlier was to issue an edict of religious toleration called the Edict of Milan,[3] which put an end in the West to the persecutions of Christians by the Roman government, making peace, so to speak, between the state and the church. This happened in AD 313.

Approximately twelve years later Constantine was deeply disturbed to discover that the major bishops and the churches under them in his recently acquired eastern empire were fighting among themselves over the teachings of a priest in Alexandria named Arius. Constantine wanted to make peace between the churches in the East, much as he had made peace between the state and the church in the West, for by this time, the church had become a powerful force in the culture. After some minor efforts to reconcile the differences between the opposing groups

3. For the text of the Edict of Milan, see §250 in *A New Eusebius: Documents Illustrating the History of the Church to AD 337*, ed. J. Stevenson and W. H. C. Frend (Grand Rapids: Baker Academic, forthcoming).

failed, a universal council was called to meet at Nicaea in AD 325. Nicaea was near some of Constantine's royal residences, so the emperor himself would be able to participate in the council. All the bishops in the world were invited, with the state paying for their transportation to make the journey. There is no accurate record of how many attended, but their number has been placed from 220 to more than 300. Almost all were from churches in the Greek-speaking East. Constantine's main goal was to unify his empire. The council was to take up all the subjects that were dividing the church, such as the date on which to celebrate Easter, some minor problems limited to Egypt, and issues concerning the clergy and the liturgy. The major issue to be discussed and settled, however, was the question raised by Arius about the relationship between the Father and the Son. The council was to arrive at a settlement that would be acceptable to the church universal.

The council of bishops produced a creed that was signed by almost all of the bishops in attendance. Probably all of the churches from which they came already had rules of faith, or baptismal confessions that were used regularly in their worship, and were more or less unanimous in what they stated, though they had never worked out one single way of expressing the faith shared by all the churches. These statements of faith would have provided the basics with which the bishops worked at Nicaea. But they had to state certain points more precisely and explicitly to show the error of what Arius was teaching.

The creed of Nicaea begins by stating the existence of two distinct beings: "We believe in one God the Father . . . and in one Lord Jesus Christ."[4] These two beings, nevertheless, share some essential elements that unify them. The creed provides some very precise definitions of the Son. The description of

---

4. See the Nicene Creed in ch. 3. The creed printed there is the revised version of the creed produced at the next ecumenical council, which met fifty-six years later in Constantinople. The part of the creed that was revised or added begins with the statement about the Holy Spirit and continues to the end of the creed. For the text of the creed as formulated at Nicaea in 325, see §291 in *A New Eusebius*.

Christ as "the only begotten Son of God, begotten by the Father before all ages, light from light, true God from true God, begotten, not made, of the same substance with the Father" defined the relationship between the Father and the Son in a way that denied the teachings of Arius. The phrase "of the same substance with the Father" was meant to contradict the Arian teaching that the Son did not share the Father's substance but had been created out of nothing. The Arians could have accepted the phrase "begotten by the Father" because they used "begotten" to mean "made." But the insertion after this of the phrase "of the same substance with the Father" defines "begotten" in such a way that the Arians could not accept it. "Of the same substance with the Father" was the key phrase in the creed that made it unacceptable to anyone holding the views of Arius. This phrase asserts the full deity of the Son. It means that whatever characterizes the Father also characterizes the Son. The Son is God, just as the Father is God, but they are two distinct beings.

The Council of Nicaea did not end the Arian controversy. The debate dragged on for decades. Nicaea did, however, define the relationship between Father and the Son in the way that was to be accepted as definitive by the majority in the church. The Council of Nicaea did not determine for the first time ever that Jesus Christ was to be considered divine. The church had believed that from its earliest days. In the Letter to the Philippians, written by Paul around the middle of the first century AD, he refers to Jesus Christ as being "in the form of God" and being "equal to God" (Phil. 2:6), and another letter from approximately the same time refers to "all the fullness of deity" being present in Christ (Col. 2:9). This is not the place to argue for the early date of Christians thinking and speaking of Christ as divine. That evidence is scattered throughout the Christian literature of the first four centuries. The Council of Nicaea did not come up with the idea that Jesus Christ should be considered divine as God the Father is divine. What the council was searching for and finally decided on was a way to express that view, already long held in the churches, with precision and clarity.

Does it make any difference whether one holds Arius's view of Christ or the view—stated as that of the majority of the churches—that was expressed in the creed of Nicaea? Athanasius, who was perhaps the strongest defender of the creed of Nicaea, provided two important answers to that question. To look in detail at these answers would take us into subjects that will be treated in later chapters of this book. But, in brief, Athanasius saw two areas where it made a tremendous difference whether one held the view of Arius or that of Nicaea. The first pertains to Christ's redemptive work. Humanity must be freed from death. Only God can overcome death. The Christ of Arius could not save us from death because the Christ of Arius is a creature and not God.[5] The other area where Athanasius saw it making an important difference whether one thought Christ was God or a creature made by God was in Christian worship. He noted that Christians worshiped Christ as God, but if Christ were not God, as Arius argued, they were worshiping a creature, which is condemned throughout the Bible as idolatry. If Christ was in reality one of the created beings, Athanasius argues, "he would not be worshiped, nor would" the exalted things said about him in the Bible "be said of him. But now, since he is not a creature, but a distinct offspring of the substance of the God who is worshiped, and is a Son by nature, he is worshiped and believed to be God."[6] How one thinks of Christ does make a difference.

Points for Discussion

1. What Scriptures might provide support for some of Arius's views?
2. How does Arius's doctrine of the Son differ from that of Theodotus and Paul of Samosata (see ch. 5)?
3. Do you think the Nicene Creed accurately portrays the way Christ is presented in the Bible? Provide some specific

5. See Athanasius, *On the Incarnation of the Logos.*
6. See Athanasius, *Against the Arians*, Oration 2, 26.23–24.

examples from both the creed and the Bible to support your answer.

4. The Nicene Creed is the creed most used in the worship of churches around the world today. Do you think this ancient statement is still an adequate expression of Christian faith? Why or why not?

Resources for Further Reading

Athanasius. *De Synodis*. In *NPNF*, 2nd series, vol. 4, *St. Athanasius*. See 451–580.

———. *Four Discourses against the Arians*. In *NPNF*, 2nd series, vol. 4, *St. Athanasius*. See 306–447.

Kelly, J. N. D. *Early Christian Doctrines*. 2nd ed. New York: Harper & Row, 1960. See especially 223–51.

Young, Frances M. *From Nicaea to Chalcedon*. 2nd ed. Grand Rapids: Baker Academic, 2010. See especially 40–72.

8

Truly God and Truly Man

Defining the Nature of Jesus

> Who, being in the form of God, . . . emptied
> himself, and took the form of a slave, when he
> came to exist in the likeness of human beings.
>
> Philippians 2:6, 7

Identifying the Major Personalities

Nestorius: A monk associated with the views of the church at Antioch. He was appointed bishop of the capital city, Constantinople, in AD 428. He was later removed from this position by the ecumenical council that met at Ephesus in AD 431, accused of teaching heretical doctrines about Christ.

Cyril of Alexandria: Bishop of Alexandria from AD 412 to 444; considered to be a major figure in framing the christological view that came to be regarded as orthodox. He was a violent opponent of Nestorius's views and was the key person in bringing about the condemnation of Nestorius's doctrine and his removal from church office.

There were two common assumptions connected with the concept of deity in the ancient world. One was that a divine being is not susceptible to suffering, and the other was that a divine being is immortal—that is, incapable of dying. God the Father had always been considered divine and, therefore, immortal and insusceptible to suffering. The creed of Nicaea made explicit that the Son is also divine. The crucial phrase in the creed that denies the truth of Arius's doctrine is that the Son is "of the same substance as the Father," which must mean that the Son, too, is immortal and insusceptible to suffering. But the Nicene Creed also says that the Son "was made flesh . . . , was crucified for us under Pontius Pilate, and suffered and was buried." The suffering and death of Jesus Christ, as we will see in a later chapter, was a vital part of the whole Christian message. Because of these conflicting concepts of deity and humanity, and the assumption that both were present in Jesus, it was inevitable that the subject of the nature of Jesus Christ would become a central point of discussion not long after the Nicene Creed had been accepted as the formal statement of what Christians believed.

It is important to understand how people of that time thought about human nature itself. A human being was understood to consist of two parts, the physical body and a nonphysical component referred to either as soul or spirit, with no difference of meaning intended between the two latter terms. We might today call this nonphysical component the mental and emotional aspects of a human being. The ancient Greeks usually called anything that was not physical "spiritual." "Physical" referred to what was perceptible by the five senses, "spiritual" to what was not. Thought, and the process of thinking, was spiritual, as were emotions. What was physical alone was not considered to constitute a real human being. The physical nature had to be joined with a soul (usually referred to as a rational soul) in order to be a human being.

Much of the fourth-century debate about the nature of Jesus Christ depends on the concepts used to describe the incarnation in the prologue of the Gospel of John. There John uses the Greek term *logos*, which is translated "Word" in most English Bibles, to refer to the divine being who was with God in the beginning and later became flesh in the person of Jesus of Nazareth. John says clearly that the "*Logos* was God" and that "the *Logos* became flesh" (John 1:1, 14). When the persons on both sides of the argument speak of God being joined with a body, or being born of Mary, or suffering, or dying, it is this divine *Logos* to which they are referring, not God the Father as some of the monarchians argued earlier.[1] How is it possible to unite the divine and the human in one human being, as the prologue to John's Gospel says they were, and what are the implications of doing this?

Two approaches were taken to define how the divine and human are related in Christ. These two approaches were centered in two prominent churches, one in Alexandria in Egypt and one in Antioch in Syria. Both sides in the debate agreed that Christ was divine as well as human. The differences lay in how they explained the relationship of these two distinct natures in the one person of Jesus Christ. We will look at the chief representative of each of the two schools of thought, as their names are often associated with these understandings, and conclude by considering the solution proposed and accepted by the Council of Chalcedon in AD 451. Nestorius is the representative figure for the approach taken at Antioch, and Cyril of Alexandria for that taken at Alexandria.

Nestorius and Cyril on the Nature of Christ

The controversy between the two opposing schools seems to have been ignited by a disagreement about how the Virgin Mary should be described. It had been rather common in the church for some time to refer to Mary as *Theotokos* (Bearer or Mother of God), a christological concept meaning that the infant Mary gave birth to was divine. Nestorius opposed the use of this term, though there is some evidence that he was willing to allow it if its usage was properly safeguarded. Some

1. See ch. 5.

opponents of *Theotokos* wanted to call Mary *Anthrōpotokos* (Bearer of Man) because, they argued, a human could not give birth to anything but a human. Mary gave birth, they argued, to the physical body of Jesus, not to the divine *Logos* that dwelled in this body. Nestorius's preferred term to describe Mary was *Christotokos* (Bearer of Christ). He argued that the eternal God, who is without beginning and without end, could not have spent nine months in a woman's womb and been born. On the other hand, what was born of Mary was not simply a human being. The term *Christotokos*, he thought, embraced both aspects of the nature of Christ.

Cyril, however, was adamant that Mary was, and was to be called, *Theotokos*. Nestorius's view, he argued, assumed that there was only a superficial joining of the *Logos* to a normal man. This, he believed, struck at the central purpose of the

---

Cyril of Alexandria on the *Theotokos*

I am amazed that there are some who are extremely doubtful whether the holy Virgin should be called Mother of God or not. For if our Lord Jesus Christ is God, then surely the holy Virgin who gave him birth must be God's mother. . . . This mystery of the incarnate Word has some similarity with human birth. For mothers of ordinary people, in obedience to the natural laws of generation, carry in the womb the flesh which gradually takes shape, and develops through the secret operations of God until it reaches perfection and attains the form of a human being: and God endows this living creature with spirit, in a manner known only to himself. . . . The condition of flesh is very different from that of spirit. But although those mothers are only the mothers of bodies belonging to this world, still they are said to give birth, not to a part of a person but to the whole person, consisting of soul and body. . . . If anyone maintained that anyone's mother was "mother of flesh" and not "mother of soul," he would be talking nonsense. For what she has produced is one living being, a composite of two dissimilar elements, but a single human being, with each element retaining its own nature.

Cyril of Alexandria, *Letter 1 to the Monks of Egypt*, in *The Later Christian Fathers*, ed. and trans. H. Bettenson (London: Oxford University Press, 1970), 252 (translation modified)

Nestorius on the *Theotokos*

Does God have a mother? Then the heathen may be excused when they introduce mothers for their gods. . . . Mary did not give birth to God, my friends. For what is born of the flesh is flesh, and what is born of the Spirit is spirit. . . . The creature did not give birth to the creator; she gave birth to a man, the instrument of deity. The Holy Spirit did not create God the Word, for that which was born of her was of the Holy Spirit, but from the virgin the Holy Spirit framed a temple for God the Word in which he should dwell.

Nestorius, Sermon 1; quoted in Cyril of Alexandria, *Five Tomes against Nestorius* (Oxford: James Parker & Co., 1881), li–lii (translation modified; available online at http://www.ccel.org/ccel/pearse /morefathers/files/cyril_against_nestorius_00_intro.htm)

---

incarnation, which was to save humanity from sin and death. If the divine *Logos* was only superficially associated with a normal human being, the work of redemption was emptied of its power, for only God could save from sin and death. Behind this controversy over the way to describe Mary lay the divided views of the Christian communities of Antioch and Alexandria over how to understand the nature of Jesus Christ.

Nestorius's teaching about Christ has been labeled a "two-natured" Christology. He was concerned to maintain a strict distinction between the divine and the human in Christ. Each nature must remain what it is without any mixture between the two. A mixture of the two natures would have produced a third kind of being, neither divine nor human. No mixture meant that each nature partook of the experiences that characterized either humanity or deity but did not cross over to experiences proper only to the other. It was the human nature in Christ, for example, that was born, suffered, and died. The divine nature was incapable of participating in any of these basic and inescapable experiences of human nature. The human nature could not be affected by the divine because it was considered necessary that the Christ experience life as a genuine human being in order to be able to redeem humanity. It could be thought of as cheating, for example, if the divine aspect of Christ intervened when he was tempted and empowered him to resist. This would make the statement that Christ can sympathize with our weaknesses because he has been tempted in the same ways that we have, but without sinning, meaningless (Heb. 4:15). Christ was completely human in his human nature. On the other hand, for the divine nature in Christ to suffer and die would have been impossible. This view would be a reversion to the earlier heresy of the patripassianists, who taught that Jesus of Nazareth was God the Father himself in flesh and that he suffered, died on the cross, and was buried.[2] Nestorius thought that the one-nature Christology of Alexandria involved the divine *Logos* in suffering and death.

Some of Nestorius's opponents seized on this strict division that he proposed between the divine and human in Christ and accused him of teaching that there were two Christs, or two Sons, in Jesus. Others, because of his emphasis on the humanity of Christ, accused him of teaching that Christ was a mere human being. The latter was certainly a false accusation, for Nestorius strongly affirmed that there was a divine nature in Christ as well as a human one. Even in his opposition to calling Mary *Theotokos*, he recognized that Mary's infant was more than just a human being. The validity of the charge that he believed there were two separate beings in Christ, however, is more difficult to refute. The Antiochene doctrine of Christ has been said to view the divine and human in Christ as "a partnership rather than a single personality."[3] Nestorius attempted, it seems, to define the unity of Christ as a single being by using the Greek term *prosōpon*, which refers to the external appearance of a thing. It was the term used in the ancient Greek theater of the mask worn by the actors. The mask defined or identified the character that the actor was playing. Later, it was used in theological literature to mean roughly what

2. See ch. 5.
3. G. L. Prestige, *Fathers and Heretics* (London: SPCK, 1963), 132.

Nestorius on the Unity of Christ

But I said and affirmed that the union is in the one *prosōpon* of the Messiah, and I made known in every way that God the Word was made man and that God the Word was at the same time in the humanity, in that Christ was made man in it.

Nestorius, *The Bazaar of Heracleides* 2.1; trans. G. R. Driver and L. Hodgson (Oxford: Clarendon, 1925), 143 (available online at http://www .tertullian.org/fathers/nestorius_bazaar_4_book2_part1.htm)

---

we call "person." It was rather commonly used, for example, in defining the Trinity, the formula being one substance, but three persons (*prosōpa*). Nestorius seems to have taught that there were two natures in Christ, a divine nature and a human nature, but that they were united in the one *prosōpon*. He insisted that even though he distinguished rigorously between the two natures, he nevertheless believed that Christ was a single, unified being.

Cyril's Christology, on the other hand, emphasized the unity of the person of Christ. The *Logos*, of course, existed eternally with God and, in the words of John's prologue, "was God." At the time of the incarnation—that is, the taking on of flesh—the *Logos* and the infant in Mary's womb were united into a single being. Cyril understood the taking on of flesh to mean a body and soul, in other words, a complete human being. The body of the infant Jesus was the body of the *Logos*. Mary was truly *Theotokos*, Bearer or Mother of the divine *Logos*. The body of the baby Jesus was not a human nature separate from the divine one. The two natures were one in Christ from the conception. They were not, however, mixed together in any way. The divine nature and the human nature were, and continued to be, different and distinct. Cyril compared it to the unity of flesh and soul in a normal human being. They were conceived to be quite different and to perform different functions in a human being. For example, one could run and the other could think. But neither nature could do anything apart from the

---

Cyril of Alexandria on the Unity of Christ

This, I think, is why the holy evangelist said that the *Logos* of God became flesh, so that one might behold at the same time the wound and its medicine, the sickness and the physician, what has been laid down in death and the one who raises to life, what has been conquered by corruption and the one who expels corruption, what has been mastered by death and the one who is more powerful than death, the one deprived of life and the provider of life. And he does not say that the *Logos* came into flesh, but the *Logos* became flesh, so that you might not think that it is as the *Logos* was in the prophets or as he visited any other saints in an incidental way, but he truly became flesh, that is human. . . . For this reason he is also God by nature in flesh and with flesh . . . , as is said in the prophet Isaiah, "Lofty men will pass over to you and will be your servants . . . and they will worship you, and pray to you, because God is in you, and there is no God but you" [Isa. 45:14]. Behold, they say both that God is in him, not separating the flesh from the *Logos*, and again they confidently affirm that there is no other God but him, uniting what is borne with the *Logos*, as his very own, that is the temple [of flesh received] from the virgin, for Christ is one from both.

Cyril of Alexandria, *Commentary on the Gospel of John* on John 1:14; PG 73:160C–161A

---

other. The divine *Logos* truly became flesh, Cyril insisted. He lived among us as a being like ourselves. Did Cyril think, then, that the divine *Logos* experienced suffering and death? There was a sense in which he did, but there were limitations to how far this could be pushed.

Cyril, as all the later Alexandrian theologians, stood in the tradition of Athanasius, who had been bishop of Alexandria just after the Council of Nicaea and had strongly defended the Nicene Creed against the Arians. Human beings, Athanasius believed, had become enslaved to death through the work of the devil. The purpose of the incarnation was to undo the work of the devil and free humanity from the grip of death. The real problem to be overcome in human redemption is not sin but death, the consequence of sin. Athanasius's theology, reduced to its lowest common denominator, is that if Christ is not divine he cannot overcome the problem of death. Therefore, Athanasius says, the "bodiless, incorruptible, immaterial *Logos* of God came to our region, . . . and took a body for himself not unlike ours." He made this body for himself within the Virgin and dwelled in it as in a temple. But because the *Logos* was immortal, he could not die. The body that he had taken, however, was mortal. And because this body also shared in the divine *Logos*, its death was sufficient to overcome the corruption and mortality of all humanity.[4] Did the divine *Logos* die? No. But because of the close association between the *Logos* and the physical body of Jesus, the *Logos* did, in a sense, share in the death, just as the physical body of Jesus would share in the life-giving power of the *Logos* in the resurrection.

Cyril made full use of a principle called the *communicatio idiomatum*. This means to speak of distinctive features of two different things as common to each. We have already discussed earlier in this chapter how the divine and the human were each considered to have exclusive features. The *communicatio idiomatum* means that one can speak of features that belong properly to one party as belonging equally to the other, although in fact they continue to be distinct features. Applied to Christ, this meant that because Cyril considered the divine and the human to be so intimately joined in Christ, it was proper to speak of things that could, in fact, happen to only one of the natures as happening to both in the one person of Christ. So the divine *Logos* could suffer in the flesh, and the flesh of the *Logos* could become the firstborn from the dead.

The Chalcedonian Definition of the Person of Christ

In AD 451 an ecumenical council met at Chalcedon to work out a formula for defining the nature of Christ that would restore harmony to the church. In addition to producing a statement about the nature of Christ, the council canonized some letters

4. Athanasius, *On the Incarnation of the Logos* 8, 9.

Leo the Great on the Nature of Christ

[In the incarnation] the properties of each nature and substance were preserved entire, and came together to form one person. Humility was assumed by majesty, weakness by strength, mortality by eternity; and to pay the debt that we had incurred, an inviolable nature was united to a nature that can suffer. And so, to fulfill the conditions necessary for our healing, the man Jesus Christ . . . was able to die in respect of the one, unable to die in respect of the other.

Thus there was born true God in the entire and perfect nature of true man, complete in his own properties, complete in ours. . . . He assumed the form of a servant without the stain of sin, making the human properties greater, but not detracting from the divine. For that "emptying of himself," whereby . . . the Creator and Lord of all willed to be a mortal, was a condescension of compassion, not a failure of power. Accordingly, he who made man, while he remained in the form of God, was himself made man in the form of a servant. Each nature preserves its own characteristics without diminution, so that the form of a servant does not detract from the form of God.

Leo the Great, Letter 28.3; in *The Later Christian Fathers*, ed. and trans. H. Bettenson (London: Oxford University Press, 1970), 278–79 (translation modified)

---

dealing with the christological question written by Cyril of Alexandria and by Leo the Great, bishop of Rome. Leo's letter (also called his *Tome*) set forth the more balanced position that had been arrived at in the Latin-speaking church. Its sentiments are often echoed in the formula produced at Chalcedon.[5]

The Chalcedonian formula for understanding the nature of Christ begins by reaffirming agreement with the Nicene Creed. Christ is, it states, of one substance with God the Father, but he is also of one substance with humanity and is like humanity in every way except for sin. He was born of the Virgin, who is referred to as *Theotokos*, from whom he received his human nature. It emphasizes that the Christ was revealed in two natures, which were not mixed together but at the same time could not

---

5. For a translation of Leo's *Tome*, see §241 in *Creeds, Councils and Controversies*, 3rd ed., ed. J. Stevenson (Grand Rapids: Baker Academic, 2012), 387–96.

The Chalcedonian Definition

Wherefore, following the holy Fathers, we all with one voice confess our Lord Jesus Christ one and the same Son, the same perfect in Godhead, the same perfect in manhood, truly God and truly man, the same consisting of a reasonable soul and a body, of one substance with the Father as touching the Godhead, the same of one substance with us as touching the manhood, *like us in all things apart from sin*; begotten of the Father before the ages as touching the Godhead, the same in the last days, for us and for our salvation, born from the Virgin Mary, the *Theotokos*, as touching the manhood, one and the same Christ, Son, Lord, Only-begotten, to be acknowledged in two natures, without confusion, without change, without division, without separation; the distinction of natures being in no way abolished because of the union, but rather the characteristic property of each nature being preserved, and concurring into one Person and one subsistence not as if Christ were parted or divided into two persons, but one and the same Son and only-begotten God, Word, Lord, Jesus Christ; even as the Prophets from the beginning spoke concerning him, and our Lord Jesus Christ instructed us, and the Creed of the Fathers has handed down to us.

From §246 in *Creeds, Councils and Controversies*, 3rd ed., trans. C. A. Heurtley (Grand Rapids: Baker Academic, 2012), 405–6

be divided or separated. The divine nature retained its divine qualities and the human its human ones, but they formed one person (*prosōpon*) and one substance.

Points for Discussion

1. Define, in your own words, the problem concerning Christ faced by the Christian thinkers of the fourth century.
2. Make a list of statements in the New Testament that refer to or suggest each of the natures of Christ.
3. Do you prefer the viewpoint of Nestorius, Cyril, or Chalcedon? Why?
4. State your own understanding of the deity and humanity of Christ.
5. Is it important that Christ is understood as both human and divine? Why?

Resources for Further Reading

Bettenson, H., ed. and trans. *The Later Christian Fathers*. London: Oxford University Press, 1970. See especially 252–62.

Cyril. *Five Tomes against Nestorius*. Oxford: James Parker & Co., 1881. See especially the preface. Also available at http://www.ccel.org/ccel/pearse/morefathers/files/cyril_against_nestorius_00_intro.htm.

Kelly, J. N. D. *Early Christian Doctrines*. 2nd ed. New York: Harper & Row, 1960. See especially 310–43.

Leo the Great. *Tome* (= Letter 28). In *NPNF*, 2nd series, vol. 12. Also available at http://www.ccel.org/ccel/schaff/npnf212.ii.iv.xxviii.html.

Nestorius. *The Bazaar of Heracleides*. Translated by G. R. Driver and L. Hodgson. Oxford: Clarendon, 1925. See especially Book 2, part 1. Also available at http://www.tertullian.org/fathers/nestorius_bazaar_4_book2_part1.htm.

Young, Frances M. *From Nicaea to Chalcedon*. 2nd ed. Grand Rapids: Baker Academic, 2010. See especially 288–321.

9

"And in the Holy Spirit"

The Struggle to Understand the Spirit

> The Spirit searches all things, even the depths
> of God. . . . And no one knows the depths of
> God except the Spirit of God.
>
> 1 Corinthians 2:10–11

Identifying the Major Personalities

Irenaeus: Bishop of Lyons, France, in the late second century; exponent and defender of the economic doctrine of the Trinity.

Tertullian: Christian writer in Carthage, North Africa, in the early third century; exponent and defender of the economic doctrine of the Trinity.

The Cappadocian Fathers: Three bishops in Cappadocia (modern central Turkey) in the fourth century—Basil of Caesarea, Gregory of Nyssa, and Gregory of Nazianzus—who were influential in defining the view of the Holy Spirit and the Trinity that became the orthodox doctrine on the subject.

There are three great festivals in the Christian year: Christmas, Easter, and Pentecost.[1] Christmas celebrates the incarnation of

1. Pentecost was a Jewish festival celebrated in the Old Testament period as a kind of harvest home festival. After the outpouring of the Holy Spirit on this

the Son of God; Easter celebrates the resurrection of Jesus; and Pentecost celebrates the outpouring of the Holy Spirit on the disciples of Jesus. This latter action was in fulfillment of Jesus's promise to his disciples, and it inaugurated and empowered the Christian mission. In the early centuries of the church, the celebration of Pentecost was characterized by joy. The fifty-day period between Easter and Pentecost was sometimes spoken of as one great festive day. Fasting was prohibited. Everything was focused on joy and celebration. But when we place Pentecost in a list with Christmas and Easter, it becomes obvious that the modern church, at least in the West, treats it as a poor relative in the family of the drama of salvation. It certainly does not rank with Christmas or Easter in the attention it receives today. Churches do not experience an exceptionally large attendance on Pentecost Sunday, as they may on Easter Sunday. There are few people in the Western world who are unaware of Christmas. But there are many, even among Christians, who are unaware of Pentecost. The day comes and goes without them knowing anything about it. This neglect of Pentecost is symptomatic, in my opinion, of the ambivalence many churches today have toward the subject of the Holy Spirit.

In the Christian tradition of which I am a part, the Holy Spirit has occasionally been considered a bit suspect. He has been thought of as problematic rather than as a cause for rejoicing and celebration. Other modern Christian traditions revel in the Holy Spirit and suspect that persons who have not experienced particular manifestations of the activity of the Holy Spirit in their lives are not Christians. Several years ago, in a class about early Christian theology, I assigned an essay on a treatise written by Tertullian about the persons of the Trinity. The students described Tertullian's arguments in the treatise very well, but when I pressed the question of whether his arguments were convincing, their faces clouded. One student's reply summed up the issue. "Perhaps," he said, "Tertullian did as well as can

---

day (Acts 2), the church adopted the day as a Christian festival to commemorate the giving of the Holy Spirit.

be done. The relationship between the Father, Son, and Holy Spirit is very difficult for us to understand."

Questions and opposing views about the Holy Spirit are not new. The early Christians also found it difficult to understand the Holy Spirit and to develop a doctrine of the Holy Spirit. Of the doctrines of the three persons of the Trinity, that of the Holy Spirit was the last to be fully developed and approved. It was not until the late fourth century that the church was more or less agreed on what it believed about the Holy Spirit. The original creed drawn up at the Council of Nicaea in AD 325 affirmed belief in the Holy Spirit but said nothing more about it. The words about the Holy Spirit in the Nicene Creed that are recited by Christians today were added to the original creed by the first ecumenical council of Constantinople in AD 381.[2] The indecision about the doctrine of the Holy Spirit and his relation to the Father and the Son is reflected in the words of Gregory of Nazianzus, a fourth-century orthodox Christian bishop, who remarked that a person could be considered orthodox if he were only slightly in error about the Holy Spirit.[3] In the fifty-six years between the councils of Nicaea and Constantinople, the question of the relation of the Holy Spirit to the Father and the Son became intense. Is the Spirit also God?

The Holy Spirit had been a part of the church's proclamation of the gospel from the very beginning. When the early Christians told the story of Jesus, they spoke of the Holy Spirit in connection with many of the key events in Jesus's life. Jesus's birth is attributed to the Holy Spirit.[4] At his baptism the Holy Spirit descends on Jesus like a dove.[5] He is said to return from his baptism in the Jordan "full of the Holy Spirit" and to be led by the Spirit into the wilderness where he is tempted.[6] He then returns to Galilee "in the power of the Spirit" to begin his

2. See the Nicene Creed in ch. 3.
3. Gregory of Nazianzus, Oration 21.33.
4. Luke 1:35; Matt. 1:18.
5. Luke 3:22.
6. Luke 4:1.

Isaiah's Servant and the Spirit

Here is my servant, whom I uphold, my chosen, in whom my soul delights; I have put my spirit upon him; he will bring forth justice to the nations. He will not cry or lift up his voice, or make it heard in the street; a bruised reed he will not break, and a dimly burning wick he will not quench; he will faithfully bring forth justice. He will not grow faint or be crushed until he has established justice in the earth; and the coastlands wait for his teaching.

Isaiah 42:1–4 (NRSV)

The spirit of the Lord God is upon me, because the Lord has anointed me; he has sent me to bring good news to the oppressed, to bind up the brokenhearted, to proclaim liberty to the captives, and release to the prisoners; to proclaim the year of the Lord's favor, and the day of vengeance of our God; to comfort all who mourn.

Isaiah 61:1–2 (NRSV)

---

ministry.[7] Jesus uses the words of Isaiah 42:1–4 and 61:1–2 to introduce and explain his ministry. Both passages speak of God putting his Spirit on his servant.[8] By doing this Jesus is claiming to be that servant to whom God has given his Spirit. On the day of Pentecost following the resurrection of Jesus, his disciples are the recipients of a powerful outpouring of the Holy Spirit.[9]

Throughout the New Testament writings the Holy Spirit is said to speak through the prophets of the Old Testament and through the apostles of Jesus. He is associated with the Father and the Son in the baptismal formula in which baptism is to be done "in the name of the Father and of the Son and of the Holy Spirit."[10] Peter refers to the Spirit as a gift given to the persons who are baptized.[11] The Spirit, in turn, is said by Paul to give the church gifts, such as wisdom, knowledge, faith, and miraculous powers, including the ability to heal, to prophesy, to distinguish

---

7. Luke 4:14.
8. Matt. 12:18–21 and Luke 4:18.
9. Acts 1:4–5; 2:1–17.
10. Matt. 28:19.
11. Acts 2:38.

Irenaeus on the Spirit as Wisdom

We have often demonstrated that the Word—that is, the Son—was always with the Father. But he says that Wisdom too, which is the Spirit, was with him before the whole creation, in the words of Solomon, "God founded the earth by Wisdom, and prepared the heaven by understanding. By his knowledge the depths burst forth, and the clouds spread dew" [Prov. 3:19–20]. And again he says, "The Lord created me as the beginning of his ways among his works; before the ages he founded me, in the beginning before he made the earth, before he established the depths, before the fountains of waters burst forth, before the mountains were made firm, before all the hills he begot me" [Prov. 8:22–25]. And again, "I was with him when he prepared the heaven, and when he made the fountains of the deep firm, I was with him fitting things together. I was the one with whom he rejoiced, and every day in all time I was glad in his presence, when he rejoiced at the completion of the world and took delight in the sons of men" [Prov. 8:27–31].

Irenaeus, *Against Heresies* 4.20.3

---

between spirits, to speak in tongues, and to interpret what is said by those speaking in tongues.[12] Paul characterizes the Christian life as a life lived by the Spirit[13] and connects the Spirit with the hope of the resurrection when he says, "If the Spirit of him who raised Jesus from the dead dwells in you, he who raised Christ from the dead will give life to your mortal bodies also through his Spirit that dwells in you" (Rom. 8:11 NRSV). There is a rich and diverse teaching about the Holy Spirit in the New Testament, but there is no explanation given of the Spirit or of the Spirit's relationship to the Father and the Son. The activity of the Spirit was simply assumed in the life of the earliest church.

The Holy Spirit Considered in Relation to His Function

The first attempts to provide an explanation of the Holy Spirit speak of the function of the Spirit in connection with the

12. 1 Cor. 12:7–11.
13. Gal. 5:16.

functions of the Father and the Son. This approach is referred to as the economic view. The word "economic" in this context has no relationship to our modern use of words such as "economy," "economics," and so forth. It refers to God's plan for the salvation of humanity. We will consider this way of understanding the Holy Spirit as presented by Irenaeus and Tertullian.

Irenaeus teaches that the Spirit was with God before the creation. He asserts that the Word, which he identifies with the Son, was always with the Father and that Wisdom, which he identifies with the Spirit, was likewise with the Father before the creation. The statement about Wisdom being with God before the creation is drawn from Proverbs 3:19 and 8:22. The identification of Wisdom with the Holy Spirit is a conclusion drawn by Irenaeus.[14] He refers to the Word and Wisdom, or the Son and the Spirit, as God's two hands. This is an important concept for him, for he presents God's works as always performed by the two together. They do not always do the same things, but the work of one complements or completes that of the other.

It is these two hands of God that perform the work of creation. He attributes this doctrine to the "rule of truth," which is probably a reference to an early summary of Christian doctrines more usually called the rule of faith. "But we hold," he says, "to the rule of truth—that is, that there is one God almighty who created all things by his Word and formed and made all things to exist from nothing, just as Scripture says, 'For by the Word of the Lord the heavens were made firm and by the Spirit of his mouth all their power.'[15] . . . Without exception the Father made all things by him. . . . He did not create through angels or other powers separated from his thought, for the God of all things needs nothing. He made all things by his Word and his Spirit."[16] The first human being was also formed in the likeness of God

14. Irenaeus, *Against Heresies* 4.20.3.
15. Ps. 33:6. In both Greek and Hebrew the same word means "spirit" and "breath."
16. Irenaeus, *Against Heresies* 1.22.1.

Irenaeus on the Hands of God

For Adam never escapes the hands of God, to whom the Father says, "Let us make humanity in our image and likeness" [Gen. 1:26]. For this reason, in the end it is "not from the will of the flesh nor the will of man [John 1:13]," but from what pleases the Father that his hands have perfected the living human being, so that Adam might be made in the image and likeness of God.

Irenaeus, *Against Heresies* 5.1.3

"by his hands—that is, by the Son and the Spirit, to whom he also said, 'Let us make humankind.'"[17]

It is through these same two hands that the Father works in salvation. The Spirit prepares a person for the Son, the Son leads the person to the Father, and the Father grants eternal life.[18] In connection with the work of the two hands of God in the creation of humanity, Irenaeus sees a parallel work in the consummation. The first Adam was corrupted and was expelled from paradise. In the final times the Word and the Spirit of God again are united with the substance of Adam's formation and make humanity alive again and receptive of the Father. The two hands of God make Adam over in the image and likeness of God.[19]

Note from these examples that the economic approach to the Father, Son, and Spirit that Irenaeus took speaks of their respective work or activities and not about their relation to one another apart from that of their activities. Tertullian, writing a few years later than Irenaeus, anticipated much of the vocabulary and form that the orthodox doctrine of the Holy Spirit and the Trinity would take in the fourth century. He provided the vocabulary, in fact, that was used in the Western, Latin-speaking church when it formulated a full doctrine of the Trinity. That doctrine itself, however, was first worked out in the Eastern, Greek-speaking church.

17. Irenaeus, *Against Heresies*, 4.Preface.4; cf. 4:20.1.
18. Irenaeus, *Against Heresies* 4.20.5.
19. Irenaeus, *Against Heresies* 5.1.3.

Tertullian on the Trinity

We believe that there is only one God, but under this dispensation, which we call the economy, we believe that there is a Son of the one only God, his Word, who proceeded from him, by whom all things were made and without whom nothing was made. We believe that this Son was sent by the Father into the virgin and was born of her, both man and God, Son of man and Son of God, and named Jesus Christ. We believe that he suffered, was put to death and was buried, according to the Scriptures, and was raised by the Father and taken up into heaven to sit at the right hand of the Father, to come again to judge the living and the dead. From heaven, in keeping with his promise, he sent from the Father the Holy Spirit, the Paraclete, the sanctifier of the faith of those who believe in the Father, the Son, and the Holy Spirit. We believe that this rule (of faith) has come down to us from the beginning of the gospel, preceding even the first heretics.

Tertullian, *Against Praxeas* 2

Tertullian asserts that the Son has his source from the substance of the Father. The Spirit, in turn, proceeds from the Father through the Son.[20] Later, in the same work, he attempts to explain the relationship between the three persons by analogies. He compares the relation between the Father and the Son to that between the root and the tree, the fountain and the river, and the sun and the ray of light that comes from it. While the tree is not separated from the root, he argues, it is nevertheless proper to call them two. And so it is also, he argues, with the Father and the Son. Then he adds the Holy Spirit to his analogy. The Spirit, he says, is related to the Father as the fruit of the tree is third removed from the root, or as the stream that flows out of the river is third from the fountain, or as the apex of the ray is third removed from the sun. Each, however, has all the properties that belong to the original source from which it is derived. "In the same way," he argues, "the Trinity, flowing down from the Father through intertwined and connected steps, does not at all disturb the Monarchy [that is, that there is only

---

20. Tertullian, *Against Praxeas* 4.

one God], while at the same time it preserves the economy [that is, the separate functions of each member]."[21] The analogies are a bit strained when Tertullian adds the third element, but the point he is trying to make is clear: both the Son and the Holy Spirit have their source in the substance of the Father. It is proper, therefore, to speak of the three as one. But it is also possible to speak of them as three without destroying the unity of the Trinity. The three, he argues, are inseparable yet distinct from one another. They are one in substance, but three in form.[22]

The Holy Spirit in Relation to the Father and the Son

Many questions about the Holy Spirit came up in the fourth century, some as the result of the Arian controversy, whose focus was on the deity of the Son.[23] The creed of Nicaea was silent about the deity of the Holy Spirit. Scripture did not call him God in so many words, nor did the liturgical practices of the church provide instances of worship or prayer addressed to the Holy Spirit.

It was not immediately obvious even to all who accepted the Nicene understanding of the deity of Christ that the Holy Spirit should likewise be understood as fully divine. Not long past mid-century, Athanasius wrote several letters to Bishop Serapion of Thmuis, who had asked him how to respond to those who denied the full deity of the Spirit.[24] A little later, Gregory of Nazianzus says that some of his opponents asked, Whoever has worshiped or prayed to the Spirit, and where is it written that such should be done?[25] Some in the fourth century who held the orthodox view of the Father and the Son claimed that the Holy Spirit differed from them in that he was a created

21. Tertullian, *Against Praxeas* 8.
22. Tertullian, *Against Praxeas* 9; 2; see also 25.
23. See ch. 7 above.
24. See C. R. B. Shapland, *The Letters of St. Athanasius concerning the Holy Spirit* (London: Epworth, 1951).
25. Gregory of Nazianzus, Oration 31.12.

Gregory of Nazianzus on the Spirit

[W]e have such confidence in the Godhead of the Spirit, that . . . we shall begin our theological exposition by applying identical expressions to the Three. "He was the true light that enlightens every man coming into the world"—yes, the Father. "He was the true light that enlightens every man coming into the world"—yes, the Son. "He was the true light that enlightens every man coming into the world"—yes, the Comforter. There are three subjects and three verbs—he was and he was and he was. But a single reality was. There are three predicates—light and light and light. But the light is one, God is one. . . . If there was a "when" when the Father did not exist, there was a "when" when the Son did not exist. If there was a "when" when the Son did not exist, there was a "when" when the Holy Spirit did not exist. If one existed from the beginning, so did all three.

Gregory of Nazianzus, Oration 31, *On the Holy Spirit* 3–4; in *On God and Christ*, trans. L. Wickham, Popular Patristics Series 23 (Crestwood, NY: St. Vladimir's Seminary Press, 2002), 118–19

---

being and was distinguished from the angels only in degree. The three Cappadocian bishops—Basil of Caesarea, Gregory of Nyssa, and Gregory of Nazianzus—insisted that the Holy Spirit was not a created being but had existed from all eternity in conjunction with the Father and the Son and shared full deity with them.

An important line of argument in the Cappadocians' claim that the Holy Spirit is divine just as the Father and the Son are divine was that all three are spoken of in Scripture as performing the same works. The descriptive titles used of the Father and the Son in Scripture are also applied to the Holy Spirit, with the exception of the begotten/unbegotten contrast that distinguishes the Son from the Father. The term "begotten" was considered to apply to the Son exclusively and the term "unbegotten" to apply exclusively to the Father. Otherwise, in Scripture terms are applied without distinction among the three, and this application of divine titles to the Spirit, it was argued, amounted to an assertion of the Spirit's deity. The Holy Spirit is God, the Cappadocians argued, because he does what only God can do.

Gregory of Nyssa on the Spirit

The Father and the Son and the Holy Spirit in like manner sanctify and quicken and enlighten and comfort, and all such things. And let no one attribute in a special manner to the activity of the Spirit the power of sanctifying, when he has heard the Saviour in the Gospel say to the Father regarding the disciples: "Father, sanctify them in thy name." And likewise too all other things are performed equally among the worthy by the Father and the Son and the Holy Spirit—every grace and virtue, guidance, life, consolation, change into immortality, passing into freedom, and whatever other blessings there are that come down to us.

Basil, Letter 189 (usually attributed to Gregory of Nyssa); in Saint Basil, *The Letters*, trans. R. J. Deferrari, LCL (Cambridge, MA: Harvard University Press, 1962), 3:65

The Spirit, Gregory of Nazianzus claims, is the cause of the birth of Christ from the Virgin, precedes the Christ as forerunner, descends on the Christ at his baptism, leads the Christ into the wilderness temptations, and takes the place of Christ when Christ ascends. "Is there any significant function belonging to God," Gregory asks, "which the Spirit does not perform? Is there any title belonging to God, which cannot apply to him, except 'unbegotten' and 'begotten'?"[26]

The Cappadocians also faced the problem of distinguishing the three persons as well as uniting them as deity. These fathers shared a common approach to this problem. They distinguished between the general and the particular in relation to the Father, Son, and Holy Spirit. While each of the Cappadocian fathers used slightly different ways of expressing it, the common approach they took drew on the analogy of the distinction between being human and being a particular human being. All human beings share the common feature of humanity, but each one is a particular manifestation of that humanity. Basil, for example, says, "The godhead is general; the fatherhood is particular.

---

26. Gregory of Nazianzus, Oration 31.29, in *On God and Christ*, trans. L. Wickham, Popular Patristics Series 23 (Crestwood, NY: St. Vladimir's Seminary Press, 2002), 139, translation modified.

We must bring them together then by saying, 'I believe in God [that is, the general concept of deity] the Father [the particular manifestation of deity]." The same combination of terms must be used in confessing the Son and the Holy Spirit: "I believe in God the Son," and "I believe in the divine Spirit, the holy one."[27]

We will let Gregory of Nazianzus have the final word. Some had raised the dilemma of whether to conceive of the Holy Spirit as an unbegotten or a begotten being. If the first, they argued, then there are two unbegotten beings, the Father and the Holy Spirit, and the Father's uniqueness in this respect is gone. But if the Spirit is begotten, then he must have been begotten by either the Father or the Son, and if it was the Father, then there are two sons. Gregory, in effect, rejects this dilemma and asserts that begotten and unbegotten are not the only alternatives for explaining the origin of the Holy Spirit. Jesus, in fact, referred to the Holy Spirit as "*proceeding* from the Father."[28] This, Gregory argues, is a middle term between being unbegotten and being begotten and differs from each. "The Son," he says, "is not Father; . . . yet he is whatever the Father is. The Spirit is not Son. . . . Yet whatever the Son is, he is. The three are a single whole in their Godhead and the single whole is three in personalities."[29] He draws a rather good analogy for this complicated subject by looking at the creation of humanity. Adam was "molded by God"; Eve was a portion taken from Adam; and Seth was their offspring. Each of the three humans came to exist in a different way, but they were all of the same substance. They were different individuals with a different means of origination, but they were the same substance. Both Eve and Seth came from Adam, but they were not both his offspring. One was a portion of him, and the other was his offspring. Nevertheless, their identity was the same. They were all three human beings.[30]

27. Basil, Epistle 236.6; in *The Later Christian Fathers*, trans. H. Bettenson (London: Oxford University Press, 1970), 78.
28. John 15:26.
29. Gregory of Nazianzus, Oration 31.29, in *On God and Christ*, 122–23.
30. Gregory of Nazianzus, Oration 31.11, in *On God and Christ*, 124–25.

The fact that three individuals all share in being human does not guarantee, however, that they will always agree with one another, or that they will ever agree with one another. The Cappadocians recognized this. But it was believed that there was always complete harmony among the three persons of the Trinity. Gregory of Nyssa, in particular, calls attention to this deficiency in the argument. He considers it simply an inadequacy of the model, because the divine persons are completely united in will and action. No action is ever done by one member of the Trinity, he argues, without the full assent and cooperation of the other two members.[31] The view of the Holy Spirit and his relationship to the Father and the Son expressed by the Cappadocian fathers, as three individual beings sharing a common substance with a unity of will and action, became the accepted orthodoxy in the succeeding ages of the church.

Points for Discussion

1. Explain the difference between the way Irenaeus and Tertullian approached the doctrine of the Trinity and the way the Cappadocians did so.
2. What do you consider the strongest argument for understanding the Holy Spirit as deity alongside the Father and the Son?
3. How is Pentecost celebrated in the church you attend?
4. Do you think the economic view of the Trinity or the view proposed by the Cappadocian fathers is more helpful/accurate? Why?

Resources for Further Reading

Bettenson, H., ed. and trans. *The Later Christian Fathers*. London: Oxford University Press, 1970. See sections on the Holy Spirit and the

31. Gregory of Nyssa, *On Not Three Gods*, *NPNF*, 2nd series, vol. 5 (Grand Rapids: Eerdmans, 1983), 331–36.

Trinity under Basil of Caesarea, Gregory of Nazianzus, and Gregory of Nyssa.

Gregory of Nazianzus. *On God and Christ*. Translated by F. Williams and L. Wickham. Popular Patristics Series 23. Crestwood, NY: St. Vladimir's Seminary Press, 2002. See the Fifth Theological Oration (Oration 31).

Gregory of Nyssa. *On Not Three Gods*. In *NPNF*, 2nd series, vol. 5. Also available at http://www.ccel.org/fathers.html.

Tertullian. *Against Praxeas*. In *ANF*, vol. 3. Also available at http://www.ccel.org/fathers.html.

Wilken, Robert Louis. *The Spirit of Early Christian Thought*. New Haven: Yale University Press, 2003. See especially 80–109.

10

God the Father

"Maker of Heaven and Earth"

In the beginning God made the heaven and
the earth. And the earth was invisible and unformed, and darkness was above the abyss,
and the Spirit [or wind] of God was moving
above the waters.

Genesis 1:1–2 (Septuagint)

Identifying the Major Personalities and Sources

Irenaeus: Bishop of Lyons, France, in the late second century AD.

Plato: Greek philosopher of fourth-century BC Athens.

Aristotle: Greek philosopher of fourth-century BC Athens.

Tertullian: Christian writer in Carthage, North Africa, in the early third century AD.

Stoics: A school of philosophers originating in the third century BC and very popular in the early Christian period.

All creeds of the church refer to God the Father as creator of
all things. The earliest such statement, which comes from the

Shepherd of Hermas in the middle of the second century, says, "First of all, believe that God is one, who created and put all things in order, and made all things to exist from what did not exist" (*Herm. Mand.* 1.1).[1] The first statement in the Nicene Creed is "We believe in one God, the Father almighty, maker of heaven and earth, of all things visible and invisible."[2] The belief in God as creator of the universe was basic to early Christian doctrine. The triune God alone was without beginning. All other things had a beginning in the creative power of God the Father. One point the early Christians argued about, however, was whether God created all things from nothing, a doctrine referred to by the Latin phrase *creatio ex nihilo*, or whether he created by bringing order to a formless, preexisting material. The doctrine of *creatio ex nihilo* is stated explicitly in the creedal statement from the *Shepherd of Hermas* quoted above. We will examine what the early Christians said about this controversial point in this chapter, focusing both on what in the biblical evidence might allow these divergent interpretations and on the philosophical views of the origin of the universe that were popular in that period that influenced the thinking of some Christians. Finally, we will consider why some of the early Christians thought it was important to hold that creation had been *creatio ex nihilo*.

Creation in the Bible

Everything said about creation in the Bible is derived from the opening chapters of Genesis, especially Genesis 1. The repeated appearance of the word "God" in this chapter is noticeable even to a casual reader. Genesis 1 shows that everything that exists, from the heavenly bodies to the smallest creatures on the earth, was made by God. God spoke, and things came into existence.

---

1. See also Irenaeus, *Against Heresies* 3.4.2; Tertullian, *Prescription against Heresies* 13; *On the Veiling of Virgins* 1.3; *Against Praxeas* 1.1–2.
2. See ch. 3 above.

When the first two verses of Genesis, however, are pressed for an answer to the question "Did God create from nothing, or from something?" the answer is less clear. The King James Version of the Bible, which has been followed by most English translations of these two verses, has "In the beginning God created the heaven and the earth. And the earth was without form, and void; and darkness was upon the face of the deep." This rendering would favor *creatio ex nihilo*. But the New Revised Standard Version of the Bible has "In the beginning when God created the heavens and the earth, the earth was a formless void and darkness covered the face of the deep." This translation, which is also a possibility from the Hebrew text, allows one to think that there might have been a formless, chaotic void from which God produced the formed earth. This would mean that there was a preexisting material out of which all things were made. This difference depends on where one puts the full stop in the sentence. Should the opening words of Genesis be read as one statement, as in the NRSV, or two, as in the KJV? If they are read as two statements, then one is faced with the problem of explaining why the chaos (Gen. 1:2) is referred to as existing *after* the creation of heaven and earth.

The Old Testament scholar Gerhard von Rad has argued that the opening words of Genesis should be read as two statements. He acknowledges that both readings of the text are possible. But, he argues, Genesis 1 asserts that God, in his freedom, has established a beginning "for absolutely everything."[3] Von Rad also argues that the Hebrew verb "to create" used here suggests *creatio ex nihilo* because it is never used elsewhere in the Old Testament in connection with making something from material.[4] The Jewish translators of the Hebrew Genesis into the Greek of the Septuagint, however, appear not to have thought there was anything special about this verb, for they translated it with the common Greek verb "to make," rather than with the less

---

3. Gerhard von Rad, *Genesis*, trans. J. H. Marks (Philadelphia: Westminster, 1961), 46.

4. Von Rad, *Genesis*, 47.

frequently used verb "to create."[5] This ambiguity in the first two verses of Genesis 1 opened the door for various understandings of how God created.

The most frequent thing said of creation in other passages in the Bible is that it was the result of the command or word of God.[6] This, of course, is based on the repeated statements in Genesis 1, "And God said. . . . And it was so." Sometimes God's hand is referred to as creating, and sometimes his will is.[7]

In the New Testament the *Logos* or the Christ is sometimes mentioned as the agent through whom God created.[8] Biblical authors sometimes refer to creation when they want to speak of God's power and greatness[9] or God's providential control of history.[10]

One can argue that by implication creation is understood in the Bible to be creation out of nothing, but there is no explicit statement of this in the Bible itself. The explicit doctrine of *creatio ex nihilo* was developed in the second century AD. Before we take that up, however, we need to see what the philosophical schools thought about the subject of creation, for this too played a role in the church's understanding.

The Understanding of Creation in the Philosophical Schools

There were three views of creation among the philosophical schools. One, held by Aristotle and his disciples, was that the universe has always existed. It had no beginning. Consequently, these philosophers had no doctrine of creation. The universe did not come into existence from some beginning or as the result of some power. It was always present.

5. See the quotation of Genesis at the beginning of this chapter.
6. Pss. 33:6, 8–9; 148:5; Rom. 4:17.
7. Isa. 48:13; 45:12; Rev. 4:11.
8. John 1:3; Col. 1:16.
9. Rom. 1:20; Isa. 40:18–28.
10. Isa. 45:12; 48:13; Acts 4:24; Rev. 10:6.

Philo on Creation

Moses . . . could not fail to recognize that the universal must consist of two parts, one part active Cause and the other passive object; and that the active Cause is the perfectly pure and unsullied Mind of the universe, . . . while the passive part is in itself incapable of life and motion, but when set in motion and shaped and quickened by Mind, changes into the most perfect masterpiece, namely this world.

Philo, *On the Creation of the World* 8–9; in *Philo*, trans. F. H. Colson and G. H. Whitaker, LCL (Cambridge, MA: Harvard University Press, 1962), 1:9–11

Plato and his followers, on the other hand, believed that the universe originated from a creative divine action. Plato discusses creation in his *Timaeus*. He calls God "the maker and father of this universe" and describes the act of creation as God bringing order out of disorder.[11] He calls material that which "is visible" and says that God brought order out of the disorderly movement of what was visible.[12] This concept of creation in Plato became the central point for discussing creation among his later followers, whether pagan, Jewish, or Christian. It was understood to mean that God performed his creative work on previously existing material.[13]

The doctrine of creation held by Stoics was similar to Plato's to the extent that they too thought that a divine power had worked on previously existing material. The Stoics believed that there were two principles in the universe, one active and called variously God, *Logos*, Spirit, or fire, and one passive, which is material substance. The active principle acts upon the passive, bringing form and life to it. Both principles were believed to be eternal. Like Plato, the Stoics taught that God created from a preexisting eternal material.

Some philosophical Jewish authors shortly before the time of Christ and also in the first century of the Christian era adopted

11. Plato, *Timaeus* 28c; 30a.
12. Plato, *Timaeus* 30a.
13. See Cicero, *On the Nature of the Gods* 1.19.

Plato's understanding of the creation. The author of the Wisdom of Solomon speaks of God's "almighty hand," which "created the world from formless matter," and the Jewish philosopher Philo of the first century AD, in his treatise *On the Creation of the World*, speaks of God imposing order on that which was without order.[14] Later in the same work, Philo echoes the Stoic doctrine of creation when he says that the universe consists of an active cause and a passive object. He calls the active cause the mind of the universe. This mind gives life to the passive element and shapes it into the world.[15]

Christian Discussion of Creation prior to Tertullian

The views that God created the universe out of nothing and that he created it from preexisting material were both present among Christians at Rome in the middle of the second century. In the *Shepherd of Hermas*, God is twice described as creating from nothing. One reference is the statement quoted at the beginning of this chapter. The other speaks of God creating that which exists out of that which does not exist—that is, from nothing.[16] No argument is given to support the assertion in either passage. It is presented as an accepted fact. The author may have been dependent on the statement in the Jewish document 2 Maccabees, where it is asserted that God made nothing in heaven or earth from things that existed.[17]

The opposite view is expressed by Justin Martyr in his *First Apology*, also written at Rome in the middle of the second century, and is clearly dependent on Plato. "We have been taught," Justin says, "that God created all things . . . from formless matter."[18] Justin thought that Plato had taken his doctrine that God made the universe from unformed matter from Moses. He

14. Wis. 11:17; Philo, *On the Creation of the World* 21–22.
15. Philo, *On the Creation of the World* 8–9.
16. *Herm. Vis.* 1.1.6.
17. 2 Macc. 7:28.
18. Justin, *1 Apology* 10.2.

> ### Theophilus of Antioch on Creation from Nothing
>
> What would be remarkable if God made the world out of preexistent matter? Even a human artisan, when he obtains material from someone, makes whatever he wishes out of it. But the power of God is revealed by his making whatever he wishes out of the non-existent.
>
> Theophilus, *To Autolycus* 2.4, in Theophilus of Antioch, *Ad Autolycum*, trans. Robert M. Grant (Oxford: Clarendon, 1970), 27

understood the first two verses of Genesis to tell both how and from what God made the universe. He understood Genesis 1:2 to speak of the underlying matter from which God, by his word, created the whole universe.[19] Justin was never considered heretical. Justin's student Tatian modified Justin's doctrine and taught that God first created matter and then created the universe by imposing order on this unformed matter he had already created.[20]

The Greek philosophical view, however, which taught that creation involved bringing order out of chaos or imprinting form on unformed material, assumed that the formless material had always existed. Theophilus, the Christian bishop of Antioch in the last quarter of the second century, insisted on the doctrine of *creatio ex nihilo* against the Greek philosophical views. He argues that if God created by using an eternally preexisting material then that material was equal to God.[21] Near the end of the second century Irenaeus, bishop of Lyons, proposed a similar argument. He says that while human beings can make things only from material that already exists, God has demonstrated his superiority to humanity by calling into existence the substance of creation itself when it had no previous existence.[22] The statements from these later authors show that as the second century drew to its conclusion the view that God created the universe

19. Justin, *1 Apology* 59.
20. Tatian, *Oration to the Greeks* 12.1.
21. Theophilus, *To Autolycus* 2.4.
22. Irenaeus, *Against Heresies* 2.10.4.

from nothing was becoming more important. In the following section we will see Tertullian insisting on this doctrine.

Tertullian against Hermogenes on Creation

Hermogenes was a late second-century Christian whose views on creation were considered to be heretical. Theophilus of Antioch, mentioned above, wrote a treatise specifically against him.[23] We do not know what Theophilus attacked in this treatise, for it has not survived. Tertullian wrote a treatise specifically against Hermogenes's doctrine of creation, which we will consider below. Hippolytus, writing a little later than Tertullian in the third century, has a brief chapter about Hermogenes in his *Refutation of All Heresies* in which he attacks Hermogenes's doctrine of creation. Hippolytus notes, however, that on other doctrines that were basic to the Christian faith, Hermogenes believed what other Christians believe. Hermogenes recognized Christ to be the Son of the God who created all things; and he acknowledged Christ to have been born of a virgin, and later crucified and raised physically from the dead, and to have ascended into heaven.[24] It appears that it was his views on the creation alone that caused him to be considered a heretic.

According to Tertullian, Hermogenes used both logical and scriptural arguments to support his doctrine of creation. He argued that God must have created the universe out of himself (which was logically impossible), out of nothing (which would make God the creator of evil), or out of something.[25] It appears that Hermogenes was concerned to prevent God from being blamed for the origin of evil. He also argued that if God was always God, he must also have always been Lord. This demanded the existence of something over which he was Lord, and this,

23. Eusebius, *Ecclesiastical History* 4.24, refers to it and says the title was *Against the Heresy of Hermogenes*.
24. Hippolytus, *Refutation of All Heresies* 8.17 (8.10 in *ANF* 5:122–23).
25. Tertullian, *Against Hermogenes* 2.1.

> ## Hippolytus on Hermogenes
>
> Hermogenes . . . said that God made all things from matter that was coeternal and uncreated. For, he said, God could not have made the things that were created out of that which did not exist. He added further that God is always Lord and always maker, and matter is always servant and in process of being created, but not all matter. For while matter was continually moving in a wild and disorderly manner, God marshaled it with his word. When he saw matter boiling like a molten stream aflame he divided it and took one part and tamed it, but permitted the other to continue its disorderly movement. The tamed part, Hermogenes says, is the universe, and the part that remains wild is called disorderly matter. . . . But he confesses Christ to be the son of the God who created all things, and further, to have been born of the virgin and the Spirit, in accordance with the word of the gospel. He also acknowledges that after his passion Christ was raised in the body, appeared to the disciples, and ascended into heaven.
>
> Hippolytus, *Refutation of All Heresies* 8.17

Hermogenes asserted, was matter.[26] Matter, therefore, must have always existed.

Hermogenes argued that the words "beginning" in Genesis 1:1 and "earth" in Genesis 1:2 refer to matter. Further, he argued, the use of the word "was" in reference to earth in Genesis 1:2 indicates its eternal existence. That means that "earth," which he understood to mean matter, did not "come to be" but always "was." Hermogenes claimed that the adjectives "invisible" and "unfinished" (in the Septuagint translation) used of the earth, meaning matter, referred to the chaotic condition of matter prior to the creation.[27] He also said that matter was neither good nor evil, so that both good and evil things could be made from it.[28] Hermogenes's doctrine depended on the Platonic philosophical doctrine of creation from preexisting matter, but he attempted to wed it to the Genesis creation account, as Justin and Tatian had attempted before him.

26. Tertullian, *Against Hermogenes* 3.1.
27. Tertullian, *Against Hermogenes* 23.1.
28. Tertullian, *Against Hermogenes* 37.1

Tertullian enters into detailed arguments against each of the assertions of Hermogenes. These can be passed over, but we will look at what is his most basic, positive argument for the doctrine of *creatio ex nihilo*. This argument rests on the Jewish and Christian doctrine that there can be no other God than the one God. God must have created from nothing, he says, because there was nothing before him. All things are posterior to God because "all things are by him." And all things are by him because "they are from nothing."[29] The argument, which sounds rather circular, draws on an assumption that Tertullian does not express, but that, as we saw above, Theophilus of Antioch did express. This is the view that if matter is coeternal with God then it is, in a sense, divine itself, making two eternally existing divine beings. But if the Jewish and Christian doctrine of only one God is true, then this possibility is nullified. And Tertullian stood firmly for the first article of all Christian creeds: "We believe in one God, the Father."

Tertullian also admits that Scripture does not state explicitly that creation was from nothing. But, he says, it also does not state explicitly that it was from preexisting material. There is less necessity, however, to state that all things were made from nothing than to state that they were made from something that preexisted. The very fact that there is no mention of a source from which something is made suggests, he thinks, that it was made from nothing. On the other hand, if an object is made from something but the source is not specified, two misunderstandings are possible. First, one might conclude that it was made from nothing. This would be incorrect. Or one might imagine the source material to have been something very different from what it actually was. It would have been necessary, Tertullian reasons, for Scripture to state that the world was made from preexisting material, had this been the case, to avoid misconceptions of the creation. Therefore, the fact that Scripture does not name the material from which the

29. Tertullian, *Against Hermogenes* 17.

creation was made supports the view that creation was from nothing.[30]

Perhaps a simple illustration will clarify Tertullian's argument. Think of God as a contractor and the world as a house he constructs. If he makes the house without using any material, there is no need to add that the house was made from nothing. But if he makes it from the finest material available, importing the highest-quality marble and cedar for the construction, he would want to point this out so that no one would think it was made from nothing at all or from cheap local lumber and artificial stone. Since, therefore, nothing is said of "building material" in the Genesis account of creation, Tertullian reasons, this absence of information suggests that there was none.

The ambiguity of Scripture on the question of whether God shaped and ordered preexisting matter when he created or whether he created all things from nothing allowed earlier Christians such as Justin to interpret Genesis 1 in a way that was in harmony with the best philosophy of his day. These philosophical views, however, came to be considered unacceptable in the late second century, for they were thought to carry with them the possibility of admitting the existence of a second, eternal divine being unrelated to the Christian God. From that time forward, advocating the doctrine of *creatio ex nihilo* became one of the touchstones of adhering to acceptable doctrine.

Points for Discussion

1. Gather and list as many statements about creation as you can from the Bible.
2. What do these statements tell you about creation?
3. Do you think the arguments for *creatio ex nihilo* or those for God shaping preexisting matter are more convincing? Why?

30. Tertullian, *Against Hermogenes* 21.

4. Do you think a particular view of creation should be used to evaluate the legitimacy of a person's Christian faith? Why?

5. Would Hermogenes be accepted as a Christian in the church you attend? Why?

Resources for Further Reading

Kelly, J. N. D. *Early Christian Doctrines*. 2nd ed. New York: Harper & Row, 1960. See especially 83–87.

Plato. *Timaeus*. In *The Collected Dialogues of Plato*. Translated by B. Jowett. Edited by E. Hamilton and H. Cairns. Bollingen Series LXXI. New York: Pantheon, 1961.

Tertullian. *The Treatise against Hermogenes*. Translated and annotated by J. H. Waszink. Ancient Christian Writers 24. New York; Ramsey, NJ: Newman, 1956. Also in *ANF*, vol. 3, and online at http://www.ccel.org/fathers.html.

Theophilus of Antioch. *Ad Autolycum*. Edited and translated by R. M. Grant. Oxford: Clarendon, 1970.

11

Binding the Strong Man

The Redemptive Work of Christ

How can one enter the strong man's house
and plunder his goods unless he first bind the
strong man?

Matthew 12:29

Identifying the Major Personalities

Irenaeus: Bishop of Lyons, France, in the late second century.

Origen: Christian teacher in Alexandria and Caesarea in the third century.

Athanasius: Bishop of Alexandria in the fourth century.

John Chrysostom: Bishop of Constantinople in the fourth century.

Gregory of Nyssa: Bishop of Nyssa in Cappadocia in the fourth century.

Ambrose: Bishop of Milan in the fourth century.

Augustine: Bishop of Hippo, North Africa, in the fifth century.

Cyril of Jerusalem: Bishop of Jerusalem in the fourth century.

The subject of this chapter stands at the center of the Christian faith. All doctrine has its ultimate raison d'être in the redemptive work of Christ. The Nicene Creed recognizes this, though it is easy to miss in a casual reading. The central portion of the creed states that Christ "*because of us humans and because of our salvation*, came down from heaven and was made flesh by the Holy Spirit and the Virgin Mary, and became incarnate" and "was crucified *for us* under Pontius Pilate, and suffered and was buried, and was raised on the third day in accordance with the Scriptures, and . . . ascended into heaven and is seated at the right hand of the Father."[1] I have italicized the words that speak directly of the work of Christ, but everything in the section is connected with this subject—that is, the references to the incarnation, crucifixion, resurrection, and ascension of Christ. Christ came to earth to carry out the work of human redemption.

There are three major ways the redemptive work of Christ has been understood by Christians. One is associated with Abelard, who lived in the twelfth century. This view is often referred to as the *subjective view* of redemption. It looks particularly at the cross of Christ as the revelation of God's overwhelming love for humankind. He loved so deeply that he sent his son to die for humanity. As a result of this demonstration of God's love, human beings are attracted to him. In this interpretation redemption is thought of as affecting human beings. This is why it is called the subjective view. A different view prevailed, however, in the Middle Ages. Anselm of Canterbury, who lived in the eleventh century, argued that it was God's justice that had to be satisfied. God had decreed laws specifying how people should live, but these laws had been broken by all human beings. God could not simply cancel these laws and the penalty of death that accompanied breaking them and still be just. Only the death of a perfect human being who had not broken any of God's laws and, therefore, did not need to die for his own sins

1. See the creed in ch. 3 above.

could satisfy this demand for justice. This theory is called the *satisfaction theory* of redemption. On this view Christ's work of redemption affects God.

A rather different understanding, however, prevailed as the dominant view in the classical period of Christian doctrine. Modern Christians tend to think of Christ's work of redemption in terms of providing forgiveness for their personal sins and making it possible for them to "go to heaven." This individualistic understanding is not completely in error, but it diminishes the grand scale of the work of Christ as understood in the classical period of Christian doctrine. The early Christians understood Christ to have become incarnate and come to earth to do battle with the devil and the forces of evil that hold this world captive.[2] Individual salvation was a result of this cosmic spiritual battle that involved the overthrow of Satan. Jesus's words in Matthew 12:29 were central to the understanding of the work of redemption in the accounts of many of the early Christian writers: "How can one enter the strong man's house and plunder his goods unless he first bind the strong man? Then he shall plunder his house." The "strong man" in the statement is Satan and the work of Christ was understood by the early Christians to have been to overpower him and take back those held in the bondage of sin and death under Satan's power. This classic view of the work of Christ is also referred to as the "Christus Victor" view, which means "the victorious Christ."[3]

The Christian writers of this early period did not all present this view in exactly the same way, but there are certain things that persist in their presentations. First and foremost is that in this view the work of Christ affects the devil, not God—as in the later satisfaction view—or even human beings, as they were understood to be affected in the later subjective view of redemption. In the Christus Victor view of redemption Christ

2. Gustaf Aulén established this as the dominant understanding of the work of Christ in the biblical and patristic periods in his definitive study *Christus Victor*, trans. A. G. Hebert (New York: Macmillan, 1961).

3. Aulén, *Christus Victor*, 4–7.

frees humanity from bondage to the devil. The devil holds humanity under his power by the double chains of sin and death. The patristic accounts also often suggest an element of deceit in the decisive defeat of Satan, who is considered to have been tricked into a struggle he could not win. This is thought to be just repayment because he originally gained power over humanity by his trickery in the story of the fall in Genesis 3. We will begin by looking at the teaching of Irenaeus on this subject in the late second century, and then broaden the perspective to some Christian writers in the third, fourth, and fifth centuries.

The Work of Christ in Irenaeus

Irenaeus was the earliest of the church fathers to speak explicitly of the redemptive work of Christ. He understood Christ's work in redeeming humanity to be rooted in the Genesis story of the creation and fall of humanity. In accordance with John 1:3, Irenaeus speaks of the activity of creation as being performed by Christ. He refers to humanity as Christ's "handiwork" or his "ancient handiwork."[4] The devil, however, by promising the first humans that they could be as gods, persuaded them to disobey God's command. This put them under the devil's power, which rests in human "disobedience and rebellion."[5] It was through this rebellion that the devil was able to bind humanity.

The work of redemption consisted in freeing humanity from the devil's power. Christ became flesh through the Virgin, Irenaeus says, "to undo death and work life in man; for we were in the bonds of sin, and were to be born through sinfulness and to live with death."[6] But before humanity could be freed from its bondage to sin and death, the devil himself had to be overpowered. Irenaeus draws on the imagery used by Jesus in Matthew

4. Irenaeus, *Against Heresies* 3.16.6; 3.18.1, 6; 3.21.10.
5. Irenaeus, *Against Heresies* 3.23.1; 5.21.3.
6. Irenaeus, *Proof of the Apostolic Preaching* 37, in *St. Irenaeus: Proof of the Apostolic Preaching*, trans. J. P. Smith, SJ, Ancient Christian Writers 16 (New York; Ramsey, NJ: Newman, 1952), 71.

Irenaeus on Christ's Victory over Satan

[Christ has] summed up all things, . . . waging war against our enemy, and crushing him who, at the beginning, led us away captives in Adam, and trampled on his head, as you can learn in Genesis where God said to the serpent, "And I will put enmity between you and the woman, and between your seed and her seed; he shall be on the watch for your head, and you for his heel" [Gen. 3:15]. For from that time, he who would be born of a woman, [that is] from the virgin, after the likeness of Adam, was preached as keeping watch for the head of the serpent. This is the seed of which the apostle says in the Epistle to the Galatians, "that the law of works was established until the seed should come to whom the promise was made." This is made even clearer in the same Epistle where he says, "But when the fullness of time was come, God sent forth his son, made of a woman." For . . . the enemy would not have been fairly vanquished, unless it had been a man [born] of a woman who conquered him. . . . And therefore our Lord professes to be the Son of man, containing in himself that original man . . . so that, as our species descended to death through a conquered man, so we may ascend to life again through a victorious one.

Irenaeus, *Against Heresies* 5.21.1, in *ANF* 1:548–49 (translation modified)

12:29 to describe this aspect of Christ's work. Irenaeus speaks of the work of Christ in terms of fighting and conquering the devil. By his own obedience, Christ did away with the human disobedience that had put humanity under the devil's control. "He bound the strong man, and set free the weak, and endowed His own handiwork with salvation by destroying sin."[7] This binding of the strong man resulted in his house being plundered and death being destroyed.[8] Irenaeus takes the plundering of the strong man's house to refer to Christ reclaiming and setting free the humanity the devil had held in bondage. The work of Christ resulted in the captives being set free and their former captor bound as a captive himself.[9]

Irenaeus's thought resembles, in some respects, Paul's contrast of Adam and Christ in Romans 5. Adam's disobedience, Paul

---

7. Irenaeus, *Against Heresies* 3.18.6–7, in *ANF* 1:448.
8. Irenaeus, *Against Heresies* 3.23.1.
9. Irenaeus, *Against Heresies* 5.21.3.

says, brought sin and death into the world, and these extended over all humanity; Christ's "act of righteousness" provides "justification and life." The first resulted in sin having dominion over humanity "in death"; the second results in grace having dominion, leading to "eternal life."[10] Both Paul and Irenaeus see humanity as helplessly in the grip of Satan, sin, and death but rescued and restored to life by Christ. The lines of the picture sketched out by Irenaeus depicting the work of redemption as a cosmic conflict between Christ and Satan were taken up and fleshed out by the major authors in the church in the later centuries of the classical period. We will look at what a few of these authors said.

Redemption in Third- and Fourth-Century Christian Understanding

Irenaeus seems to have thought that all the activity of Christ on earth took place as a part of the conflict between Christ and the devil. He certainly understood the narrative of the temptation of Jesus to have spoken directly of this struggle.[11] He did not restrict the battle specifically to the time of Christ's passion. Origen, on the other hand, speaks pointedly of the cross as the focal point of the conflict with Satan. "What do the demons fear?" he asks. "At what do they tremble? Without doubt, the cross of Christ in which 'they have been conquered, in which their principalities and powers have been stripped.'"[12]

Origen expresses a modification in the classic idea of redemption as we have seen it set forth in Irenaeus. Irenaeus depicted the rescue of humanity from the devil as a battle between Christ and Satan. Origen does this too, but he also speaks of a ransom transaction taking place between Christ and the devil. Although

10. Rom. 5:12–21 (NRSV).
11. Irenaeus, *Against Heresies* 5.21.2–22.2.
12. Origen, *Homilies on Exodus* 6.8 (cf. Col. 2:15); in *Origen: Homilies on Genesis and Exodus*, trans. R. E. Heine, FOTC 71 (Washington, DC: The Catholic University of America Press, 1982), 293–94. See also *Homilies on Exodus* 4.6.

> ## The Son of Man Came "to Give His Soul a Ransom for Many"
>
> [Christ came] to the human race, that he might serve, and he proceeded so far with our salvation that he gave his own soul as a ransom for many who believed in him. And if, by way of supposition, all believed in him, he would have given his soul as a ransom for all.
>
> But to whom did he give his soul a ransom for many? Certainly not to God. Was it perhaps, then, to the evil one? For the latter had power over us until the soul of Jesus was given to him as a ransom for us. He was deceived <of course and imagined> that he could have power over it. He did not see that he could not apply torture to constrain it. For this reason "death," having thought it had power over "him, no longer had power" [Rom. 6:9] over the <only> one who was free "among the dead" [Ps. 87:5 Septuagint] and stronger than the power of death. He was so much stronger that those held by death who wished to follow him were able to be free. Death no longer had any power against them at all, for death cannot assail anyone who is with Jesus.
>
> Origen, *Commentary on Matthew* 16.8

we were all created by God, he says, we each sold ourselves to the devil by our sins. In this way we became his slaves. "Christ came, however," he says, "and 'bought us back' [Gal. 3:13] when we were serving that lord to whom we sold ourselves by sinning."[13] This buying back demanded some sort of payment. The payment, Origen asserts, was the soul of Christ. He is following the biblical language of Matthew 20:28 when he speaks of Christ offering his soul as a ransom. He refuses to entertain the thought that the ransom was paid to God. It was the devil who had acquired power over human souls and was holding them in death. The dealings had to be with the devil. Jesus gave his own soul up to the devil in death. But the devil was deceived in this transaction because he thought he would then have power over the soul of Christ. But Christ was so much stronger that even the human souls held by death were able to be freed. Death lost its power over all the souls who were with Jesus. There are

13. Origen, *Homilies on Exodus* 6.9; in *Origen: Homilies on Genesis and Exodus*, 295.

echoes of Jesus's statement about binding the strong man and plundering his house in these comments of Origen, but the statement is not mentioned explicitly. Origen's understanding is, nevertheless, in the same trajectory of thought as that of Irenaeus when he spoke of the binding of the strong man.

Origen's account of Christ giving his soul to the devil as a ransom contains a hint of the deception that was involved in overcoming the devil. This became much more pronounced in later authors, as we will see. Origen himself expresses it more explicitly when he compares Christ's work of redemption to a king who disguises himself as a citizen of his enemy so that he can overcome him without a violent battle. He does not want to destroy the people ruled by his enemy because they were formerly his own people. He wants to free them. In his disguise he persuades those who formerly served him to return to his rule. "Then . . . he binds the strong man," Origen says, "and despoils his powers and principalities and leads away the captives which had been seized and were being held by the tyrant." This is what he thinks Paul is describing in Philippians 2:6–8 when he says that Christ, who had been in "the form of God . . . emptied himself and took the form of a slave . . . and became obedient unto death." By his death Christ destroyed the devil, who held the power of death, and freed those held captive by death.

> For when [Christ] had bound the strong man and triumphed over him by means of his cross, he even advanced into his house . . . of death in the underworld, and from there he plundered his possessions, that is, he led away the souls which [the devil] was keeping. This is what he was speaking about in an enigmatic way in the Gospel when he said, "Who is able to enter the house of a strong man and plunder his possessions unless he first binds the strong man?"[14]

14. Origen, *Commentary on Romans* 5.10; in *Origen: Commentary on the Epistle to the Romans Books 1–5*, trans. T. P. Scheck, FOTC 103 (Washington, DC: The Catholic University of America Press, 2001), 373–74.

Here the motif of the deception of the devil is joined with that of the binding of the strong man to present the redemptive work of Christ.

Gregory of Nyssa uses a vivid image to depict the deceit of the devil in the death of Christ. He says it was a case of the deceiver being deceived. The devil had first deceived human beings by using pleasure as bait that caught them and trapped them in death. The devil agreed to the ransom exchange because he had seen the power manifest in Christ's earthly life. He thought he would be gaining this power in exchange for those locked in the prison of death. But "it was not in the nature of the opposing power," Gregory says,

> to come in contact with the undiluted presence of God . . . , therefore, to assure that the ransom . . . would be readily accepted by him . . . , the Deity was hidden under the veil of our nature, that so, as with ravenous fish, the hook of the Deity might be gulped down along with the bait of flesh, and thus life being introduced into the house of death, and light shining in darkness, that which is diametrically opposed to light and life might vanish; for it is not in the nature of darkness to remain when light is present, or of death to exist when life is active.[15]

Consequently, when he swallowed the hook of Christ's divinity the devil was caught and those in death's prison were set free. Gregory uses multiple images in this paragraph. His first assumption is that evil cannot tolerate the presence of God. The nature of God, therefore, must have been hidden or the devil would never have approached Christ directly. The divine nature, therefore, was covered by the human nature of Christ. The devil thought he was dealing with a man, not with God. This is the fishhook imagery. The hook was the deity of Christ; the bait was the humanity that covered it. But how did the victory over Satan come about? Gregory then switches to the imagery of light and darkness. Darkness vanishes whenever light is introduced. When

15. Gregory of Nyssa, *Catechetical Oration* 24; in *NPNF*, 2nd series, 5:494.

Satan took the deity of Christ into his possession, he brought the light of God into his kingdom of darkness, which put an end to the darkness, or to Satan's kingdom. Gregory joins an allusion to life-death imagery with the light-darkness imagery. Life and death cannot coexist in the same person. The power of Satan's kingdom lay in death, which sin had introduced. But Christ is life. Therefore, when Satan brought Christ, or life, into his kingdom of death, death was vanquished.

Augustine takes a similar approach when he refers to the Lord's death as the bait in the mousetrap that caught the devil. He, too, sees this deceit of the devil as his comeuppance for trapping the first man and binding him with death. "By seducing the first man," Augustine says, "he slew him: by slaying the last man, he lost the first from his snare. . . . The Lord's cross was the devil's mousetrap."[16] In another treatise he attempts to explain how the death of Christ effected the freeing of humanity from death. When Christ was put to death, he argues, his "blood, being the blood of one who was entirely without sin, was poured out for the remission of our sins, so that whereas the devil rightly has in his power those whom he had bound under sentence of death, as guilty of sin, he should rightly lose control over them because of him on whom he had wrongly inflicted the death penalty, when he was completely guiltless. . . . In this redemption the blood of Christ was given for us as the price: but by accepting it the devil was not enriched, but enchained."[17]

In the fourth century Athanasius used the second chapter of Hebrews to talk about death in much the same way that Irenaeus and Origen had talked about the devil. Death has imprisoned humanity, Athanasius says. The author of Hebrews identifies the devil as the one who holds the power of death. Athanasius argues that it was necessary that the divine *Logos*, who created humanity in the beginning, take on flesh so that he might

16. Augustine, Sermon 261.1, in *The Later Christian Fathers*, trans. H. Bettenson (London: Oxford University Press, 1970), 222.
17. Augustine, *On the Trinity* 13.19; in *The Later Christian Fathers*, 222–23.

Hebrews on the Power of Death

Since, therefore, the children share flesh and blood, he himself likewise shared the same things, so that through death he might destroy the one who has the power of death, that is, the devil, and free those who all their lives were held in slavery by the fear of death.

Hebrews 2:14–15 (NRSV)

---

sacrifice his body to renew life in those who had fallen prey to death. "For because death gained power over human beings from human beings, the destruction of death and the resurrection of life occurred by means of the *Logos* of God becoming a human being."[18] In a later chapter he says, "But the Lord came that he might bring the devil down."[19]

In John 12:31, when Jesus is very near the time of his arrest and crucifixion and is struggling with his own feelings about his imminent suffering, he hears a divine voice affirming that the divine name will be glorified in what is about to happen. Jesus responds, "Now is the judgment of this world; now the ruler of this world will be cast out." In the late fourth century, John Chrysostom addressed these words of Jesus in a homily, saying,

> [W]hat is "the judgment of this world"? It is as though He said, "there shall be a tribunal and a retribution." How and in what way? "He [Satan] killed the first man, having found him guilty of sin (for 'by sin death entered' [Rom. 5:12]) but he did not find sin in me [Christ]. Why then did he . . . give me over to death? Why did he put into the mind of Judas to destroy me?" . . . "How then is the world judged in me?" It shall be said to Satan, as if a court of justice were sitting, "Well, you killed all people because you found them guilty of sin. But why did you kill Christ? Is it not clear that this was wrong? Therefore the whole world shall be avenged in Christ." . . . And to show that

18. Athanasius, *On the Incarnation* 10.
19. Athanasius, *On the Incarnation* 25.

this is the implication, hear what he says, "Now shall the prince of this world be cast down," "by my death."[20]

Chrysostom's view is also that Christ's redemptive work involved dealing with the devil, but he draws his imagery from the law courts. Satan is on trial for killing Christ. He had the right to kill Adam, and all humanity following Adam, because they all sinned and deserved the penalty for sin, which was death. But Christ did not sin. Satan, therefore, overstepped his rights when he killed Christ. This unjust action of Satan against Christ causes Chrysostom's imaginary law court to pronounce that the devil be dethroned and all his victims freed.

The early Christians understood the work of Christ to have freed them, in one way or another, from the power of sin and death that the devil held over humanity. Christ had bound the strong man and taken back the human property that the devil had deceptively acquired. The classic view of redemption affirms that humanity belongs not to Satan but to God, by right of both creation and redemption.

Points for Discussion

1. What is the major difference between the classic, or "Christus Victor," view of the redemptive work of Christ and the other views?
2. Make a list of statements from the New Testament that either support the classic view of redemption or suggest a different point of view.
3. Do you think the classic view is a meaningful way of understanding the work of Christ today? Why or why not?
4. How does the church you are most familiar with talk about the redemptive work of Christ?

20. John Chrysostom, *Homilies on St. John* 67.2 on John 12:31; in *NPNF*, 1st series, 14:249–50 (translation modified).

Resources for Further Reading

Athanasius. *On the Incarnation*. In *NPNF*, 2nd series, vol. 4. Also available at http://www.ccel.org/fathers.html.

Aulén, Gustaf. *Christus Victor*. Translated by A. G. Herbert. New York: Macmillan, 1961.

Ernest, James D. "Redemption." In *The Routledge Companion to Early Christian Thought*, edited by D. Jeffrey Bingham, 271–87. London and New York: Routledge, 2010.

Webber, Robert E. *Ancient-Future Faith*. Grand Rapids: Baker Academic, 1999. See chs. 5–6.

12

"I Will Build My Church"

Defining the Church

Christ loved the church and gave himself up
on her behalf.

Ephesians 5:25

Identifying the Major Personalities

Irenaeus: Bishop of Lyons, France, in the last quarter of the second century.

Ignatius: Bishop of Antioch in the early second century and author of seven letters that are extant.

Tertullian: Christian writer in Carthage, North Africa, in the early third century.

While most people would consider Jesus himself to have preceded the church, the Letter to the Ephesians in the New Testament claims that it was for the sake of the church that Jesus died (Eph. 5:25), and in the Gospel of Matthew Jesus speaks of building his church (Matt. 16:18). The concept of the church is firmly anchored in Jesus himself. In the Acts of the Apostles that group of people who gathered around the apostles of Jesus immediately after his death and resurrection is called the church (Acts 5:11). All of the letters of Paul in the New Testament, except Titus and the two letters to Timothy, are written to the churches in various cities. The Revelation to John includes letters addressed to seven churches in Asia Minor.

The church has had a major role in Christian thought from the very beginning. It must, nevertheless, be defined as it was understood in the period of what we have called classical Christian doctrine, for it has taken many different forms and has been understood in many different ways. What must be present in order for a group of people to be called the church of Jesus Christ? In this chapter I begin with a survey of what defines the church in the New Testament and then turn to the understanding of some Christian teachers in the second and third centuries. These theologians faced different situations and different problems, and these situations and problems called forth their reflections on the nature of the church. I discuss only the most distinctive contribution each of these teachers made to the understanding of the church. I conclude by considering the statement about the church in the Nicene Creed and some of its implications for understanding the church today.

Important Marks for Defining the Church in the New Testament

The first and most characteristic mark of the church in the New Testament is its faith. The earliest Christians believed what Matthew records Peter as saying to Jesus, "You are the Messiah, the son of the living God." This faith in Jesus as Messiah set the first Christians apart from their pagan contemporaries and from the Jews, with whom they shared faith in the one God of the Old Testament. The Acts of the Apostles and the Pauline epistles indicate that this faith in Jesus as Messiah was the center of early Christian preaching.

This understanding of Jesus's identity is claimed to derive directly from Jesus through the apostles. The apostle Paul praises the Corinthians because, he says, they continue the traditions just as he had passed them on (1 Cor. 11:2). The author of Hebrews is most explicit in this respect when he warns his readers about neglecting the message of Christian salvation, which, he says, "was declared at first through the Lord, and it was attested to us by those who heard him" (Heb. 2:3 NRSV). Paul castigates the Galatians for deserting the gospel he preached and turning to another gospel (Gal. 1:6–9) and asserts that he had received what he preached from a revelation from Jesus himself (1:12).

The New Testament documents indicate a unanimity in this faith in Jesus among the early Christians. J. N. D. Kelly notes that in the later books of the New Testament especially, there is a repeated emphasis on a coherent body of teaching that is handed down. Jude 3 speaks of "the faith once delivered to the saints." The author of Hebrews speaks several times of "the confession" to which one should hold fast (Heb. 3:1; 4:14; 10:23). Kelly has called attention to what he refers to as fragments of early Christian creeds that appear in several New Testament books. These fragmentary confessions of faith are always centered on Christ.[1]

A second mark considered essential to the understanding of the church in the New Testament is the presence of the Holy Spirit. The beginning of the church is associated with an outpouring of the Holy Spirit on young and old, and on men and women (Acts 2:16–18, 33, 38). Those baptized in the name of Christ receive "the gift of the Holy Spirit" (Acts 2:38). The apostles send Peter and John to Samaria to impart the gift of the Holy Spirit by "laying their hands on" converts there who have not received the Holy Spirit at their baptism (Acts 8:12–17), and Paul rebaptizes and lays hands on some disciples of John the Baptist in Ephesus who have not received the Holy Spirit (Acts 19:1–6). The whole life of the Christian can be described

1. J. N. D. Kelly, *Early Christian Creeds*, 3rd ed. (New York: Longman, 1991), 8.

as lived in the Spirit. The contrasts of flesh and Spirit or law and Spirit refer to non-Christian versus Christian ways of living (Gal. 5:4–5, 16–25).

The authentication of the presence of the Spirit is more ambiguous in the New Testament. One is assumed to have received the Spirit at baptism if it is a proper Christian baptism (Acts 2:38). But, as noted in the previous paragraph, there are alternative ways of receiving the Holy Spirit. Reception of the Spirit is linked, in general, with the beginning of the Christian life and considered essential to it. The manifestation of the presence of the Spirit might take the form of extraordinary gifts (Acts 10:44–46; 19:6; 1 Cor. 12:9–10), of more mundane gifts (Rom. 12:6–8), or of the so-called fruit of the Spirit (Gal. 5:22–23).

The most important authenticating mark of the Spirit in the church is the Spirit's testimony to Christ and his agreement with Christ. Jesus says the Spirit, which he will send on his disciples, will glorify him (John 16:14). Paul corrects some of the Corinthians who have claimed that their assertions against Jesus were made under the influence of the Spirit. He asserts that no one can speak curses against Jesus by the Spirit of God, and no one can claim Jesus as Lord apart from the Holy Spirit (1 Cor. 12:3). John also warns against false prophets who claim to speak by the Spirit. He says that only those who acknowledge that Jesus Christ "has come in the flesh" have the Spirit of God (1 John 4:2–3).

Justin Martyr on Old Testament Prophets

Certain men among the Jews . . . became prophets of God, through whom the prophetic Spirit proclaimed in advance things that were about to happen before they happened. . . . Moses, then, was the first of the prophets. . . . And Isaiah, another prophet, prophesied the same things in different words. . . . Hear where Micah, another prophet, said in advance he would be born. . . . And David, the king and prophet, who spoke these words, experienced none of them.

Justin, *1 Apology* 31.1; 32.1, 12; 34.1; 35.5

One thing that became important after the New Testament period was the association of the Holy Spirit with Scripture. This had its roots in the general view that prophets spoke under the influence of the Spirit. The early church considered not only the authors of what we call the prophetic books of the Old Testament to have been prophets but also David, Samuel, and Moses. The early church, therefore, considered most of the Old Testament to have been the writings of prophets, who spoke under the influence of the Spirit. In the New Testament the word of God is referred to as "the sword of the Spirit," and the Holy Spirit is said to speak in Scripture, meaning the Old Testament (Heb. 3:7; 9:8; 10:15).

A third mark of the church in the New Testament that set its members off from others is a particular lifestyle or discipline. The discipline that characterized Christian existence in the New Testament is difficult to define precisely, but it is quite obvious that there was such a discipline. The entire book of Jude addresses this issue, linking the perversion of Christian discipline with the perversion of Christian doctrine, a connection also made in the early third century by Tertullian. John also refers, though in an imprecise manner, to the way that Christians are expected to live. He speaks of "walking in light" as opposed to darkness and obeying Christ's commandments, though the only commandment specified is to love one's brother or sister (1 John 1:5–2:17). The teachings of Jesus, especially as embodied in the Sermon on the Mount, probably served as the accepted guide for Christian living. Paul appeals occasionally to teachings of Jesus concerning Christian discipline. Toward the end of the first or beginning of the second century, the *Didache* set forth instructions for those anticipating baptism. A large portion of these instructions come from Jesus's Sermon on the Mount (*Did.* 1–6).

Two additional markers of the church in the New Testament are its ministry and its practice of baptism and observance of the Lord's Supper. The latter two are considered as one marker, often referred to as sacraments, though that term is not used of them in the New Testament. Baptism was the initiation rite that was considered to make one a part of the body of believers called the church. I pass over further discussion of baptism now because it is the subject of chapter 13. The Lord's Supper consists of bread and wine said by Jesus at his last meal with his disciples to be his body and his blood. He commanded his disciples to eat the bread and drink the wine to remember him.[2] The church has faithfully continued to repeat this ceremonial meal from its beginning to the present.

The ministry of the church is referred to in Ephesians as an outpouring of gifts from Christ himself consequent to his ascension, which made some apostles, others prophets, others evangelists, and still others pastors and teachers (Eph. 4:7–12). These terms are all attested elsewhere in the New Testament of various people performing the ministry of the church. The term "apostle" is usually limited in the New Testament to those twelve who accompanied Jesus during his earthly life, and Paul. The other terms are used more generally. In addition, Paul is said in the Acts of the Apostles to have appointed elders or presbyters as leaders in the churches he established in various cities, and in the letters of 2 Timothy and Titus bishops, presbyters/elders, and deacons are mentioned. These latter three categories became central to the ministry of the church in later centuries.

Defining the Church in the Second and Third Centuries

I begin with Irenaeus and the importance of apostolicity—that is, a connection with the apostles—as a mark of the church. The primary problem facing the church in the time of Irenaeus, so far as its self-understanding was concerned, was gnosticism. We have already briefly discussed Irenaeus and the gnostics in chapter 1, where we considered one aspect of the gnostic teaching about Jesus. Gnostics defined the church in relation to the

2. 1 Cor. 11:23–26; Matt. 26:26–29; Mark 14:22–25; Luke 22:14–22.

> ### Irenaeus on Apostolicity
>
> True knowledge is the teaching of the apostles and of the ancient community of the church in the whole world, and the stamp of the body of Christ in accordance with the successions of bishops to whom the apostles handed down that church that exists everywhere.
>
> Irenaeus, *Against Heresies* 4.33.8

quality of the life of its members. They insisted that baptism did not make a Christian, but only the receiving of the Holy Spirit.[3] They referred to the bishops and deacons of the church as "dry canals"[4] and claimed not to need the ministry of the "shepherds" of the church but to have been taught another "hidden" way directly by Christ, who is the "true shepherd" of the soul.[5] The gnostics also claimed that profession of the creed did not make one a Christian, nor did dying for the faith in martyrdom. It is the inner life of the person, they claimed—the spiritual life and especially the spiritual understanding, which they called *gnosis*—that marks a Christian. They referred to themselves as spiritual people and to people in the church in general as "common and ecclesiastical."[6] These, of course, are very subjective criteria for defining a Christian.

The church in general rejected the subjective criteria of the gnostics and insisted instead on objective criteria that could be seen and tested for defining who was and who was not a part of the church: acceptance of the creed (that is, the common faith held by Christians), the presence of the ministries ordained and sanctioned by the apostles, the sacraments instituted by Jesus and handed on by the apostles, and obedience to the Scriptures accepted by the church as inspired by the Spirit and authoritative. These provided objective, observable criteria for

3. *Gospel of Philip* 64; in *NHL*, 139.
4. *Apocalypse of Peter* 79; in *NHL*, 343.
5. *Authoritative Teaching* 32–33; in *NHL*, 282.
6. Irenaeus, *Against Heresies* 3.15.2.

Tertullian on the Rule of Faith

The rule of faith is, indeed, completely one, alone unalterable and unchangeable. It is the rule of believing in one only God, who is omnipotent and the creator of the world, and in his son Jesus Christ, born of the Virgin Mary, crucified under Pontius Pilate, raised from the dead on the third day, received into heaven, now seated at the Father's right hand, who will come to judge the living and the dead through the resurrection of the flesh.

Tertullian, *On the Veiling of Virgins* 1

---

defining the group of people who could be called the church of Jesus Christ.

As early as the first quarter of the second century, Ignatius defined the church in relation to a legitimate ministry against some who were probably gnostics. He insists that nothing in the church should be done without the bishop and that no eucharistic service or baptism performed in the absence of the local bishop is valid. He insists that the proper ministry of bishop, presbyters, and deacons is essential for a group to use the name "church."[7] In the last quarter of the second century Irenaeus agreed fully with Ignatius's view in his argument with the gnostics. He takes Ignatius's argument a step further, however, and grounds the validity of the church's ministry, as also its teaching, in the apostles themselves. Irenaeus defines the church in relation to what he considers to be an objective, observable linkage with the apostles, who were instructed by Jesus himself.

Tertullian, like Irenaeus, appeals to apostolicity to identify the true church. Christ declared God's will to his disciples and commanded them to go and teach all nations, Tertullian asserts. The disciples preached the one faith in Jesus Christ and founded churches throughout Judea and the nations. All other churches derived their teaching from these churches founded by the apostles and are, therefore, apostolic, for everything is

---

7. Ign. *Smyrn.* 8.1–2; *Trall.* 3.1.

determined by its origin. Therefore, "all the churches are primitive and apostolic since they are all one church."[8]

Tertullian considers what he calls the "rule of faith" to contain the basic teaching of the church in summary form. He thinks this rule goes back to Christ himself.[9] He quotes it in three different treatises, never with exactly the same wording, but always with the same basic structure and content.[10] It begins with a short statement about the one God, who created all things. Then follows a longer section on the Son of God, setting forth the basic beliefs related to his birth, life, death, resurrection, ascension, sending of the Spirit, and return to judge and reward humankind. This body of doctrine, Tertullian believes, is the sine qua non of the church. To alter this rule or to depart from it is to cease to be Christian.[11]

One Holy, Catholic, Apostolic Church

The Nicene Creed contains the words "[And we believe] in one holy catholic and apostolic church." This confession makes four statements regarding the church that, in a sense, define the early Christian understanding of the church.

The Church Is One

We know the church in the twenty-first century as a fragmented body of people. The three major groups that make up those using the name "church" refer to themselves as Roman Catholic, Orthodox, or Protestant. Within the Protestant group there are numerous subgroups, such as Methodists, Anglicans, Presbyterians, Disciples of Christ, Baptists, Nazarenes, and so forth. The earliest Christians saw themselves as all part of one

8. Tertullian, *Prescription against Heretics* 20.
9. Tertullian, *Prescription against Heretics* 13; 37.
10. Tertullian, *Prescription against Heretics* 13 (cf. 36); *On the Veiling of Virgins* 1; *Against Praxeas* 2.
11. Tertullian, *Apology* 46.17.

body. They probably existed in each city in a number of different house churches, for in the beginning, before the church was a recognized legal body within the Roman Empire, Christians were not allowed to own corporate property. So they met to worship in the home of some individual who was a Christian. This, of course, limited the number of people who could be a part of any single worshiping group. In the earliest days there were probably numerous homes scattered throughout the larger cities where Christians gathered to worship. But these individual house churches did not consider themselves to constitute separate churches. Whenever Paul wrote to the Christians in a particular city he addressed not "the churches" (plural) but "the church" (singular) in that city, even though the Christians may have met in several different houses.

This concept of oneness among separately meeting churches is something that has been lost to the modern age. Churches within a particular denomination, or Roman Catholic or Orthodox churches, may have a sense of oneness within their particular group, but they usually think of those outside their particular fellowship of belief as distinct from themselves, certainly not as belonging to the same body of people to which they belong. This concept of oneness is something that Christians today need to learn from the ancient Christians. There seems little chance, however, to convince all Christians in their various groupings to give up their distinctive characteristics and unite as one church under, for example, one of the Catholic names or one of the Protestant denominational names. There have been numerous attempts to unite the churches, but they have all failed, including the extensive ecumenical movement of the mid- to late twentieth century.

Nevertheless, the church is one. It is a group of people who share a common faith in Jesus Christ and are devoted to living in obedience to his teachings. Robert Webber has suggested that Christian unity in the postmodern world will have to embrace the diversity that exists among the many different churches with each of the three major church bodies—Orthodox, Roman

Catholic, and Protestant—viewed as "various forms of the one true church . . . finding common ground in the faith expressed by classical Christianity." What the three differing groups have in common, he asserts, "is the classical Christian tradition of the first five centuries."[12] If such an approach were to be taken, the classical Christian doctrine reviewed in this book would be foundational for a church unified in its doctrine but diverse in its cultural expressions.

The Church Is Holy

"Holy" is a word that modern people often find difficult to understand. It is thought to refer to a kind of super piety that makes a person standoffish and produces a feeling of superiority. This is not, however, the meaning of the word in the Bible or in the Nicene Creed when it is applied to the church. Perhaps the story of Moses's experience at the burning bush can help us understand the meaning of "holy." When Moses sees a bush burning in the wilderness but not being consumed by the fire, he turns aside for a closer look. As he approaches the bush he hears the voice of the Lord say to him, "Remove the sandals from your feet, for the place on which you are standing is holy ground" (Exod. 3:5 NRSV). There is a sense in which all ground is holy in that it has been created by God, and a sense in which every bush, whether burning or not, is holy in that it too has been made by God. But there is an intensity of the presence of God in this particular spot at this time that makes this little plot of earth "holy ground." God is about to reveal himself to Moses and speak to him in a way that he has not spoken to him at other places or at other times.

Any thing, place, or person referred to as holy is in some sense a vehicle for the presence of God in a special intensity. The church is referred to as holy because it is a vehicle of this intensity of the presence of God. When Christians gather to

12. Robert Webber, *Ancient-Future Faith* (Grand Rapids: Baker Academic, 1999), 85, 92.

worship in a particular place, there is a sense in which that place and time become holy, for the Lord God speaks in special ways in that place and at that time. This occurs in the participation in the sacrament of the Lord's Supper. The Lord's Supper, as was noted earlier in this chapter, was instituted by Jesus himself during his last meal with his disciples. "Do this to remember me" (1 Cor. 11:24), he said. In participating in the Lord's Supper the believer experiences the presence of the Lord in a more intense manner than he or she does in other activities or at other times. The intensity of the presence of the Lord is also experienced in the reading, explanation, and application of Scripture that takes place when the church gathers to worship. And in the association with a group of fellow believers, the intensity of the presence of the Lord may be experienced in ways that do not occur in the regular activities of the week. It is because of these and similar experiences that the church is said to be holy. With fellow believers in the context of worship, the intensity of God's presence and of God's speaking is encountered in ways that are not experienced outside the community called the church.

The Church Is Catholic

The word "catholic" comes from a Latin word that means "universal." The church is not bounded by ethnic, racial, or national distinctions. Jesus said to his disciples, "Go and make disciples of all the nations" (Matt. 28:19). Jesus's first disciples were all Jewish. The religion of the Old Testament is the religion of the Jews. Jesus himself was a Jew. But Jesus says to go and make disciples not of the *Jewish* people, but of *all* the nations. Stephen Neill reminds us that "most of the religions of mankind have been local, and even tribal, in their character."[13] Jesus commissioned his disciples, however, to disregard ethnic and racial boundaries, territorial boundaries, and language boundaries and to take his teachings to all peoples. The sociologist Rodney

---

13. Stephen Neill, *A History of Christian Missions*, The Pelican History of the Church 6 (New York: Penguin, 1973), 13.

Origen on the Racial Diversity of Christianity

When you see Jews acting hatefully and in a hostile manner against Christians, know that that prophecy is being fulfilled which says, "And I will stir them up against those who are not a race" [Deut. 32:21]. For we are not a race. Some of us have become believers from one city and others from another, but never, from the beginning of the Christian faith, has a whole race adopted it. We are not a single, whole race, like the Jews or the Egyptians; we have been gathered from individual races here and there.

Origen, *Homily on Ps. 36* 1.1; in *Origen*, trans. R. E. Heine
(Oxford: Oxford University Press, 2010), 173

Stark thinks one of the reasons for the success of early Christian expansion was that it offered the Roman world a "coherent culture that was *entirely stripped of ethnicity*."[14] It simply did not matter what your race was. Neill further reminds us that of all the religions of the world only Christianity "has succeeded in making itself a universal religion." It has found a home, he says, "in almost every country in the world; it has adherents among all the races of men. . . . This is something that has never happened before in the history of the world."[15] The Christian message is for all people.

Overcoming ethnic boundaries was a major issue for the earliest Christians. The Acts of the Apostles and the epistles of Paul in the New Testament show in many passages how difficult it was for many of the first Christians, who were Jews, to accept non-Jews in the Christian community on an equal footing with themselves. It was customary for ancient peoples to think of the inhabitants of the world as made up of two groups: that to which they belonged and all others. The Jews, for example, divided the world population into Jews (themselves) and Gentiles (all others). The Greeks thought of the world as consisting of

---

14. Rodney Stark, *The Rise of Christianity* (San Francisco: HarperSanFrancisco, 1997), 213.

15. Neill, *History of Christian Missions*, 14, 15. Neill first published this statement in 1964. Today he might revise it to note the worldwide expansion of Islam.

Greeks (themselves) and barbarians (all others). But the Christians thought of themselves as embracing all peoples in one family of God. Origen takes the words of Deuteronomy that refer to God making the Hebrew people jealous of a race that was not a race and applies them to the Christians (see sidebar). Christians are not a single race, he argues, in the sense that they come from one particular race. They are instead a people drawn from many different races, but never from one race alone.

The Church Is Apostolic

We discussed the importance of the connection with the apostles in the church of the second and third centuries earlier in this chapter. Anchoring all the fundamentals of the church in apostolic teaching in the twenty-first century means that the church must accept the apostolic Scriptures as authoritative for its life and thought, participate in the sacraments ordained by Jesus in those Scriptures, and recognize the ministries set forth there. This is the ancient quality of the modern church. This is the source of its life, its roots, or, to change the metaphor, its foundation on which its reason for existing rests. When the church clings to its apostolic nature, then, as Thomas Oden has said, "Even the most recent converts . . . believe the very same truth that was attested by the earliest witnesses."[16]

Points for Discussion

1. Which of the marks of the church in the New Testament discussed above are important in the church that you know best?
2. Do the church groups with which you have been associated think of themselves as one holy, catholic, and apostolic church?

16. Thomas C. Oden, *The Rebirth of Orthodoxy* (San Francisco: HarperSanFrancisco, 2003), 30.

3. Do you think the four markers mentioned in the Nicene Creed need to be emphasized more in the modern church? Give reasons for your answer.

4. Might the concept of apostolicity mentioned in the creed help the church today to discover the oneness also mentioned there? If so, how?

Resources for Further Reading

Irenaeus. *Against Heresies*. In *ANF*, vol. 1. See especially 414–60. Also available at http://www.ccel.org/fathers.html.

Rankin, David. *Tertullian and the Church*. Cambridge: Cambridge University Press, 1995. See especially 91–110.

Tertullian. *The Prescription against Heretics*. In *ANF*, vol. 3. See 243–65. Also available at http://www.ccel.org/fathers.html.

13

"The Washing of Regeneration"

"One Baptism for the Forgiveness of Sins"

> In his mercy he saved us by the washing of regeneration and the renewal from the Holy Spirit.
>
> Titus 3:5

Identifying the Major Personalities and Sources

Didache: An early second-century manual containing practical instructions for the church.

Justin Martyr: A mid-second-century Christian apologist who taught in Rome.

The Apostolic Tradition: A church manual from the early third century ascribed to Hippolytus of Rome.

Cyprian: Bishop in Carthage, North Africa, in the mid-third century.

The Shepherd of Hermas: An apocalyptic-type document from the mid-second century.

2 Clement: A Christian homily from the mid-second century.

Tertullian: Christian writer in Carthage, North Africa, in the early third century.

The first mention of baptism in the New Testament is in connection with the ministry of John the Baptist. It is a baptism for the Jewish people related to his proclamation that the appearance of the kingdom of God is imminent (Matt. 3:2). It is referred to as "a baptism of repentance for the forgiveness of sins" (Mark 1:4). Many Jewish people are baptized by John, including Jesus. When Jesus comes to be baptized, John hesitates, but Jesus insists that the act is necessary "to fulfill all righteousness" (Matt. 3:13–15). Even though we may assume that Jesus does not need to have sins forgiven in baptism, his baptism is not an empty action. It clearly marks a crucial turning point in Jesus's life. The Spirit of God descends on him and a voice from heaven identifies him as "my beloved son" (Matt. 3:16–17). We know little about Jesus before his baptism. The baptism by John marks the beginning of Jesus's ministry. Thereafter Jesus begins to proclaim John's message of the imminent appearance of the kingdom of God (Matt. 4:17; Mark 1:15). Not much is said in the Gospels about Jesus and his disciples baptizing, but there are a few statements that make it clear that they did, in fact, do this. The Gospel of John notes that Jesus does not himself do the baptizing, but his disciples do (John 3:22–26; 4:1–2). In the final words of Jesus to his disciples in Matthew's Gospel, he instructs them to make disciples of the nations and baptize them (Matt. 28:19). The church has faithfully carried out this commission from Jesus throughout its history. Most churches practice baptism, though not always for the same reason or in the same way. In this chapter we will look at the practice and meaning of baptism in the classical period of Christian doctrine, beginning with the New Testament.

Baptism in the New Testament

After the resurrection of Jesus, the church distinguished Christian baptism from the baptism of John. The Acts of the Apostles relates a story in which Paul encounters some disciples of John the Baptist in Ephesus. He questions them and learns that they did not receive the Holy Spirit at the time of their conversion, and that they have been baptized only with John's "baptism of repentance." These disciples of John the Baptist then believe in Jesus and are baptized "in the name of the Lord Jesus." Paul lays his hands on them, and they receive the Holy Spirit (Acts 19:1–5 NRSV). This interesting story shows us that in contradistinction to John's baptism, the baptism of the church was done in the name of the Lord Jesus and resulted in the reception of the Holy Spirit, though in this instance, at least, the latter involved also the laying on of hands by Paul after the baptism. The significant point to note, however, is that Paul does not simply lay his hands on them when he learns that they have experienced only John's baptism, but he does so after the reception of baptism in the name of the Lord Jesus. This suggests that the earliest Christians understood the act of baptism to be a significant part, at least, of the reception of the Holy Spirit.

The New Testament speaks explicitly only of adult believers in Jesus being baptized. There are several references to people being baptized in the Acts of the Apostles.[1] In these stories those who are baptized have always heard and believed the apostolic preaching about Jesus being the Messiah sent by God. Sometimes it is added that they have also repented of their sins. These are all actions of adults. Some of the baptismal passages in Acts refer to children and entire households, but they do not state explicitly that children have been baptized. We will note later when infants are explicitly mentioned as being baptized by the church.

Baptism appears to have been performed in the New Testament period immediately upon a person's coming to faith in Christ.[2] All the candidates for baptism had been instructed about who Jesus was and what he had done. This instruction involved the citation of Old Testament prophecies about the

1. Acts 2:14–42; 8:5–17, 26–38; 9:1–18; 10:34–48; 16:11–15, 25–34; 19:1–5; 22:6–16.
2. See the references in the preceding note.

Messiah and relating the life of Jesus to those prophetic promises.[3] There is no specification of how long this instruction lasted. The indication is that it often involved only one session with the persons involved. It must be remembered, however, that the stories in the Acts of the Apostles represent a missionary situation. The church did not yet exist in any of the communities where the baptisms took place. The approach, as we will see, later changed somewhat when the church became an established part of various communities.

The English words "baptism" and "baptize" are borrowed from Greek words that, in their nonreligious usage, mean the submersion or dipping of something in water. The few places where a baptismal scene is depicted in the New Testament do not describe the actions of the rite itself but do refer to it occurring where there is an abundant amount of water. John the Baptist performs his baptism "in the Jordan river" (Matt. 3:6). He is said to have baptized at Aenon near Salim, "because there was plenty of water" (John 3:23). As Philip instructed the Ethiopian about Jesus, the man sees water and asks to be baptized. Both he and Philip go "down into the water," where Philip baptizes him (Acts 8:36–38). The symbolism used of baptism in the New Testament suggests that it was an immersion in water. Paul refers to it as being buried and raised with Christ and compares it to the Israelites crossing the Red Sea, where they were under the cloud and "in the sea" (Rom. 6:4; 1 Cor. 10:1–2).

In the New Testament, baptism is associated with the forgiveness of sins; the reception of the Holy Spirit; salvation; participation in the death, burial, and resurrection of Jesus Christ; and incorporation into the body of Christ on earth.[4] There are various images used to express the purpose and importance of baptism in the Pauline letters. One of the most powerful images is that of dying, being buried, and rising with Christ in the act of baptism. Paul insists that baptism marks a major

3. See, for example, Acts 2:14–42 and 8:26–38.
4. Acts 2:38; 22:16; 1 Pet. 3:21; Rom. 6:1–11; Col. 2:12; 1 Cor. 12:13.

turning point in a person's life. The way of life followed prior to baptism must be abandoned. What he calls "the body of sin" is destroyed—crucified, he says—with Christ. Life after baptism cannot continue as previously. That life is dead and buried in the water of baptism. The person who comes up from the water has been raised from the dead and lives for God in Christ Jesus (Rom. 6:1–11). In Colossians the imagery of being buried and raised with Christ in baptism is blended with that of being circumcised to describe the importance of baptism. Paul says, "You were circumcised with a circumcision not done by human hands . . . when you were buried with him in baptism, at which time you were also raised with him" (Col. 2:11–12). Baptism in the New Testament is a one-time act; it is not repeatable. Images associated with it, such as death, burial, resurrection, circumcision, and rebirth, suggest this. These are not repeatable actions or events. This, as we will see in the next section, would become a matter of great concern in the following century.

Baptism in the Second and Third Centuries

The *Didache* is one of the oldest Christian documents following the writings that make up the New Testament. In fact, it may have been written as early as the last decade of the first century. It is a manual of instruction for the guidance of the church. It includes instructions for how baptism should be administered but does not say anything about baptism's purpose. Baptism should be preceded, it asserts, by the instruction in Christian ethics contained in the first six chapters of the *Didache*. These ethical instructions are derived from the Bible, many coming from what we call the Sermon on the Mount. The person to be baptized must fast for one or two days prior to the event. The person doing the baptizing is encouraged to fast also, along with any others in the congregation who are able. Baptism is to be performed in the name of the Father, the Son, and the Holy Spirit by immersion in cold running water. If there is no cold

---

The *Didache* on Baptism

Now concerning baptism, baptize like this: . . . Baptize into the name of the Father and the Son and the Holy Spirit in living [that is, running] water. But if you do not have living water, baptize in other water. And if you are not able to baptize in cold water, do so in warm. And if neither is available, pour water three times on the person's head in the name of the Father and the Son and the Holy Spirit. The person baptizing and the person being baptized should fast before the baptism, and any others who can. But the person being baptized must fast for one or two days.

Didache 7

---

water, however, it can be done in warm; if there is no running water, it can be done in still water; if neither option is available, it can be done by pouring water three times on the head of the candidate (*Did.* 7).

There is both continuity with and divergence from the practice of baptism in the New Testament in the *Didache*. The baptismal formula agrees with that in Matthew 28:19, though some passages in the Acts of the Apostles suggest that baptism may have first been performed only in the name of Jesus (Acts 2:38; 19:5). In the *Didache*, baptism is still performed by immersion in water, though provision is made for pouring water on the head of the candidate when there is not enough water available for immersion. The instructions in the *Didache* diverge from the New Testament in suggesting that there is a period of ethical instruction before baptism and in the demand that the person being baptized fast before the baptism, along with others who might be able.

In the middle of the second century, Justin Martyr described a baptismal service. He says that those who accept the Christian message and promise to live by it pray and fast, asking God for the forgiveness of their sins, while the church prays and fasts along with them. They are taken to water, where they are "washed in the water in the name of God the Father . . . and of our Savior Jesus Christ, and of the Holy Spirit."[5] Fasting is connected with baptism, as in the *Didache*, and baptism appears still to be performed by immersion in water, since those being baptized go to where there is water and the action is described as a washing. Another document, called the *Apostolic Tradition*, coming from the end of the second century or the beginning of the third, goes into some detail in describing how baptism is performed.[6] Baptisms are usually performed on Easter Sunday. Those who are baptized have been instructed for three years prior to their baptism, though that time can be shortened if the person shows signs of more rapid advancement. The candidates are exorcised daily as the day for their baptism approaches. They have to fast on the Friday and Saturday preceding their baptism on Easter Sunday. The entire night preceding baptism is spent listening to Scripture read to them and receiving instruction. At dawn on Easter Sunday morning those being baptized remove their clothing and are baptized in the following order: small children, men, and women. Before entering the water the person being baptized renounces Satan and is anointed with the oil of exorcism. Each person is then immersed three times, each time following the confession of faith in one of the members of the Trinity. When the persons come out of the water they are anointed with the oil of thanksgiving, they dress, and they assemble with the church to celebrate the Eucharist.

Several new developments connected with the practice of baptism in the late second century may be identified, especially the strong emphasis on the preceding instructions, fasting, and the exorcism of the demonic powers. On the other hand, continuities with the earlier period are also obvious. Baptism is still performed by the immersion of a person in water, and those baptized are still primarily adults who have had extensive instruction before their baptism, though it is clear that children, at least, are being baptized as well. One thing that is certainly

---

5. Justin, *1 Apology* 61.

6. This document is ascribed to Hippolytus of Rome, though it is not certain that he was its author.

> ### Baptism in the *Apostolic Tradition*
>
> And [*when*] he [*who is to be baptized*] goes down to the water, let him who baptizes lay hand on him saying thus: Do you believe in God the Father Almighty? And he who is being baptized shall say: I believe. Let him then baptize him once, having his hand laid upon his head. And after <*this*> let him say: Do you believe in Christ Jesus, the Son of God, who was born of the Holy Spirit and the virgin Mary, who was crucified in the days of Pontius Pilate, and died, [*and was buried*] and rose the third day living from the dead and ascended into the heavens, and sat down at the right hand of the Father, and will come to judge the living and the dead? And when he says: I believe, let him baptize him the second time. And again let him say: Do you believe in <*the*> Holy Spirit in the holy church, and the resurrection of the flesh? And he who is being baptized shall say: I believe. And so let him baptize him the third time. And afterwards when he comes [*up from the water*] he shall be anointed by the presbyter with the oil of thanksgiving saying: I anoint you with holy oil in the name of Jesus Christ. And so each one drying himself . . . shall now put on their clothes, and after this let them be together in the assembly.
>
> *Apostolic Tradition* 20.12–20, in *The Treatise on the Apostolic Tradition of St. Hippolytus of Rome*, ed. Gregory Dix (London: SPCK; New York: Macmillan, 1937), 1:36–38 (translation modified)

obvious from these descriptions of baptism in the second-century church is that baptism was taken very seriously. It was not something entered into lightly by those who experienced it, nor was it something that was administered in an offhanded way by the church. Baptism was considered, as we noted earlier in the apostle Paul, to mark a major break in a person's life. The person who entered the water of baptism was making a major life commitment. The church recognized this and made it clear also to the person being baptized.

The practice of baptism was firmly established by the end of the second century, and the procedure outlined in the *Apostolic Tradition* was generally followed. Three points became more prominent in the third century. One was the baptism of infants. This seems to have been a regular practice by at least the early third century. The earliest explicit reference to the practice is in the period between AD 200 and 206, when Tertullian wrote his treatise *On Baptism.* He opposed the practice, but his remarks show that it was widely done.[7] In the mid-third century Cyprian defended infant baptism. A bishop had argued that infants should not be baptized before the eighth day, in keeping with the Jewish law of circumcision. Cyprian and several fellow bishops disagreed and concluded that baptism should not be denied to anyone, including the newly born.[8] Origen, also writing in the mid-third century, defended infant baptism as well.[9]

The second point that became more prominent in the third century involved the proper way to perform baptism. We noted above that the *Didache* made provision for pouring water on the head of a person instead of immersing the person when there was not enough water for immersion. In the third century a substitute for immersion was also allowed for those who were ill and on the point of death and had never been baptized. This was called "clinical" baptism, from the Greek word *klinē*, which means "bed." Some, however, raised questions about the efficacy of this baptism if the person recovered from the illness. They thought that one who recovered should then be baptized in the normal way—that is, by immersion. Cyprian was asked by a priest for his view on this issue. In reply, he says that each one (presumably meaning each bishop or priest) must draw his own conclusion. His own opinion is that the sprinkling of water on a person in that situation confers the full benefits of baptism. But, he adds, if anyone thinks that this is not the case, then those who recover should be baptized.[10]

The other point that became more prominent in the discussion of baptism in the third century concerned the finality of baptism. In the second century baptism was sometimes referred to as the "seal." "The seal," the *Shepherd of Hermas* says, "is

7. Tertullian, *On Baptism* 18.
8. Cyprian, Epistle 64.
9. Origen, *Homily on Leviticus* 8.3.5; *Homily on Luke* 14.5; *Commentary on Romans* 5.9.
10. Cyprian, Epistle 69.12–13.

the water. They descend . . . into the water dead, and come up living. This seal was preached to them, and they used it to enter into the kingdom of God" (*Herm. Sim.* 9.16.4). The concern was to keep the seal pure—that is, not to sin after baptism. In *2 Clement*, people who sin after being baptized are compared to runners who cheat in a race. They are disqualified and cannot receive the prize (*2 Clem.* 7.3–6). The writer of the *Shepherd of Hermas* says he has heard that one should live purely after baptism and never sin again. He later notes, however, that a person might repent once for sins committed after baptism (*Herm. Mand.* 4.3.1–2, 6). The *Didache* is more ambiguous but appears not to make quite so rigorous a demand. At the conclusion of the ethical instructions with which the document opens, the author says that anyone who can bear the "whole yoke of the Lord will be perfect," but the one who cannot should do what he can (*Did.* 6.2). In the prayer of thanksgiving to be offered at the conclusion of the eucharistic service, anyone who is holy is invited to come; anyone who is not is exhorted to repent (*Did.* 10.6). Tertullian, writing at the beginning of the third century, had a very rigoristic attitude. He argues that there is no salvation without baptism. Baptism is not, he says, like the Jewish washing ceremonies to remove daily defilements, because those washings are repeatable. Christian baptism, on the contrary, can be experienced only once. The gulf that baptism cuts in life between one's past and one's present is so deep, he argues, that it should not be undertaken until one is fully cognizant of the responsibilities it imposes and is in a reasonable position to fulfill them.[11]

Christians in the classical period of Christian doctrine took baptism very seriously. It was an act that was anchored in both the action and the command of Jesus Christ himself. It was intimately related to the central teachings regarding human salvation. It was something that could not be bypassed by anyone who wanted to be a follower of Jesus Christ. Tertullian

11. Tertullian, *On Baptism* 18.

expressed it vividly when he alluded to the symbol of the fish, which Christians used of Christ, and called Christians little fish born in water.[12]

Points for Discussion

1. List as many images used to describe baptism in the first three Christian centuries as you can.
2. What do these images teach about the early Christian understanding of baptism?
3. Do you think baptism is as central in the teaching and practice of the church today as it was in the first three centuries?
4. What important Christian doctrines were linked with baptism in the early Christian understanding?

Resources for Further Reading

Cyprian. *Epistles*. In *ANF*, vol. 5. (Epistle 69 quoted above is Epistle 75 in this translation.) Also available at http://www.ccel.org/ccel/schaff/anf05.html.

Ferguson, Everett. *Baptism in the Early Church*. Grand Rapids: Eerdmans, 2009.

Hippolytus. *The Apostolic Tradition of Hippolytus*. Available online at http://www.bombaxo.com/hippolytus.html.

Holmes, M. W., trans. and ed. *The Apostolic Fathers in English*. 3rd ed. Grand Rapids: Baker Academic, 2006.

12. Tertullian, *On Baptism* 1. The Christians used the symbol of the fish because the letters in the Greek word meaning "fish" make an acronym for the following statement: "Jesus Christ [is] Son of God [and] Savior."

14

The Christian Eschatological Hope

The Resurrection of the Dead

Thanks be to God who gives us the victory
through our Lord Jesus Christ.

1 Corinthians 15:57

Identifying the Major Personalities

Irenaeus: Bishop of Lyons, France, in the last quarter of the second century. Author of a work called *Against Heresies*.

Tertullian: Christian teacher in Carthage, North Africa, in the late second and early third centuries. Author of numerous writings defending Christian faith against pagans and against heresies. Author of a treatise called *On the Resurrection*.

Origen: Christian theologian and Bible expositor in the first half of the third century, first in Alexandria, Egypt, and later in Caesarea, Palestine. Author of numerous works exposing Scripture, the first Christian systematic theology, an important defense of Christian faith against the philosopher Celsus, and numerous other works, including a lost work, *On the Resurrection*.

"Eschatology" comes from the Greek word *eschaton*, which means "last." It treats subjects related to the end of human history. The subject of eschatology is usually put at the end of textbooks on Christian doctrine, as in this one. This may be the case because the term itself suggests that it should come at the *end* of something. Or perhaps it is relegated to the end because it is considered to be unimportant, and if interest lags before the end of the book is reached, the subject of eschatology can be neglected without serious loss. Eschatology may have gotten bad press because it is a subject that has often attracted religious quacks. As early as the second century there were those who set timetables for when the end of all things would occur. When this did not occur it caused both ridicule and hardships for the church.

Such misrepresentations of eschatology should not detract us from the importance of the subject in Christian doctrine. Eschatology involves much more than the timetable for the end of the world. In fact, it can hardly be said to involve that at all. Eschatology entails the important doctrines of the return of Christ, the resurrection of the dead, the judgment, the end of the present world order, and the future life. It entails, in other words, the Christian hope. These are speculative subjects, to be sure, but hardly more speculative than the doctrine of the Trinity or the nature of Christ. The significance of the doctrine of eschatology lies in the fact that it is *the* doctrine that lifts all other doctrines out of the realm of mere historical interest or curiosity and gives them contemporary relevance. It means that all the doctrines discussed in this book have something to do with *our own* present and future.

Our two final chapters are divided between two major eschatological subjects that called forth frequent discussion and disagreement among the early Christians. This chapter examines the subject of the resurrection of the dead. The next looks at the question of the return of Christ and whether or not a thousand-year reign of Christ with the saints on this earth is to be anticipated.

The Basis for the Doctrine of the Resurrection in the New Testament

The resurrection is foundational for the message proclaimed about Jesus throughout the New Testament. Each of the four Gospels concludes by relating the story of his resurrection. Paul, whose letters are the earliest Christian documents that we have, places the resurrection of Jesus at the center of the Christian message.[1] The preaching of the apostles related in Acts also makes the resurrection of Jesus the focal point of the Christian message.[2]

The hope for a future resurrection of believers rests on the resurrection of Jesus in the New Testament.[3] The New Testament doctrine of resurrection is ambiguous, however, about the exact nature of the resurrected state. Paul has two major discussions of the subject in his letters to the Corinthians. In 1 Corinthians 15:35 he indicates that the nature of the resurrected body is already being discussed in the church. There is much that is unclear in the answer that Paul gives, but two points are important to notice.

First, in 1 Corinthians 15, Paul compares the relationship between the body we now have and the resurrected body to that between a seed and the plant that is produced by the seed. That analogy suggests that there is a definite continuity between the two bodies, but that there is not an exact identification between them. You cannot find the seed that you planted in the plant that grows from it. On the other hand, the two are intimately connected. Paul says that "God gives it [i.e., that which is planted] a body as *he* has determined" (1 Cor. 15:38; emphasis added). The other point Paul makes in his discussion in 1 Corinthians 15 is based on an analogy between Adam and Christ on the one hand, and our present body and resurrected body on the other. Adam was made from the earth; Christ was not. Our present bodies are from the earth; our resurrected bodies will not be.

1. 1 Cor. 15:3–4; Rom. 1:4.
2. Acts 2:32; 3:15; 4:10, 33; 5:30; 10:40; 13:30; 17:3, 31; 26:23.
3. 1 Thess. 4:14; Rom. 6:5; 8:11; 1 Cor. 15:12–20; 1 Pet. 1:3.

Paul's other discussion of the resurrected state is in 2 Corinthians 4:16–5:10. Here again he speaks in metaphors and analogies. He begins by speaking of our "outer nature," which is "wasting away," and our "inner nature," which is continually being renewed. Then he relates the first to "what can be seen" and is "temporary," and the second to "what cannot be seen" and is "eternal." Next he changes his analogy and speaks of our physical bodies as an "earthly tent" that will be "destroyed," in contrast to the eternal "house" that God has prepared for us "in the heavens." He then speaks of our present earthly tent as clothing that we want to remove so that we can "be further clothed" (with the eternal clothing God has for us, he implies). Finally, he speaks of his own present condition as being "at home in the body" but "away from the Lord," and he contrasts this with his desire to "be away from the body and at home with the Lord."

In these two passages Paul conveys the assurance of the Christian hope of the resurrection, but he fails to give any clear picture of what the resurrected life will be like. One can argue from these two passages both that the resurrection will be physical and that it will not be physical. It is this ambiguity in the New Testament doctrine of the nature of the resurrection that lies at the basis of much early Christian discussion and disagreement on the subject, and we might add that this is still true. We turn our attention now to some ways the early Christians understood and interpreted this New Testament material.

Irenaeus and Tertullian against the Gnostics on the Resurrection of the Flesh

The subject of the resurrection became a storm center in the second century in the debate between orthodox Christians and gnostics. It was especially Irenaeus and Tertullian who argued for a resurrection of the body of flesh against the gnostics, who despised the material world, including the physical body. To the gnostics, the material world was not the creation of the

---

Resurrection in the Gnostic *Gospel of Philip*

[The soul] is a precious thing (and) it came to be in a contemptible body. Some are afraid lest they rise naked. Because of this they wish to rise in the flesh, and [they] do not know that it is those who wear the [flesh] who are naked. "Flesh [and blood shall] not [be able] to inherit the kingdom [of God]" (1 Corinthians 15:50). What is this which will not inherit? This which is on us. But what is this very thing which will inherit? It is that which belongs to Jesus and his blood. . . . His flesh is the word, and his blood is the Holy Spirit. He who has received these has food and he has drink and clothing.

Gospel of Philip, cols. 56–57; *NHL*, 134

---

true God but the work of a lesser being who did not possess deity at all. The production of matter, furthermore, was more or less an accident. For the gnostic, only what was immaterial or spiritual was important and good. This view of the material world and the physical body lies at the basis of their doctrine of resurrection. The goal of gnosticism was to free the spiritual element in human beings from its imprisonment in the fleshly body. People who were aware of the essentially useless and corrupt nature of flesh and lived only for the spiritual were said to be experiencing resurrection already.

Both Irenaeus and Tertullian claim that gnostics appealed to 1 Corinthians 15:50 to argue that the flesh is not saved. They also used 2 Corinthians 5:1–10 to argue that the resurrection is not physical but spiritual. In the gnostic *Gospel of Philip* the author combines 1 Corinthians 15:50 and 2 Corinthians 5:1–10 to argue for the resurrection of the soul without the accompaniment of the flesh.

In opposition to the gnostic view, Irenaeus argues that it is the interaction of flesh and Spirit that makes a living human being. Without the Spirit of God, flesh alone is dead and, in the words of 1 Corinthians 15:50, "cannot inherit the kingdom of God." He argues further that if flesh could not be saved the Word of God would not have become flesh. Human redemption was accomplished through the flesh and blood of Jesus.

> ### Tertullian on 1 Corinthians 15:37–38
>
> [The clause] "What you sow is not the body which will be" [does not permit you] to suppose that in the resurrection a different body is to arise from that which is sown in death. . . . For if wheat is sown . . . , barley does not spring up. Still it is not the very same grain in kind; nor is its nature the same, or its quality and form. . . . [B]ut does not the apostle himself suggest in what sense it is that "the body which will be" is not the body which is sown, even when he says, "But . . . God gives it a body as he wills"? *Gives it* of course to the grain which he says is sown bare. . . . Then the grain is safe enough, to which God has to assign a body. But how safe, if it is nowhere in existence, if it does not rise again . . . ? . . . For what purpose, therefore, will God give it "a body as he wills," when it already has its own "bare" body, unless it be that in its resurrection it may be no longer bare? That therefore will be additional matter which is placed over the *bare* body; nor is that at all destroyed on which the superimposed matter is put,—no, it is increased. . . . The truth is, it is sown the barest grain, without a husk to cover it, without a spike even in germ, without the protection of a bearded top, without the glory of a stalk. It rises, however, out of the furrow enriched with a copious crop, built up in a compact fabric, constructed in a *beautiful* order, fortified by cultivation and clothed around on every side. These are the circumstances which make it another body from God, to which it is changed not by abolition, but by amplification.
>
> Tertullian, *On the Resurrection of the Flesh* 52;
> *ANF* 3:585 (translation modified)

Consequently, if flesh and blood have gained life for us, it can hardly be said that they cannot inherit the kingdom of God. When Paul speaks of "flesh and blood" in 1 Corinthians 15:50, therefore, he does not mean the terms literally, but is referring to the sinful deeds of the flesh.

Tertullian argues that the flesh is good because it was created by God. Furthermore, because a human being is a union of soul and flesh, both must be raised from the dead in the interest of justice. The soul impels human action, and the flesh carries it out. Both, therefore, must be raised to receive either punishment or reward for the deeds done in this life.[4] When

4. Tertullian, *On the Resurrection of the Flesh* 14–17.

he argues against the gnostic interpretation of 1 Corinthians 15:50, Tertullian sounds some of the same notes that Irenaeus sounded. He appeals to the example of the physical resurrection of Christ as the model for our resurrection; he argues that Paul's words in 1 Corinthians 15:50 refer to the sinful nature of flesh and not to its substance; but he asserts, in addition, that flesh and blood will have to put on incorruption and immortality before they can enter the kingdom of God. Without this, they cannot enter it.[5]

On the basis of Paul's analogy of the seed and the plant in 1 Corinthians 15, Tertullian argues for the identity of the risen body with the present physical body. He supplements this analogy with philosophical arguments for the identity of substances even when they undergo change, and he argues that to be destroyed is one thing, but to be changed is another. To be destroyed is to cease to exist, but to be changed is to continue to exist although in another condition. He illustrates this with changes common to human life, such as body size, health, and age. The person continues to be the same person even though the physical, mental, economic, or social conditions may have changed radically.[6]

The view of the resurrection of the physical body taught by Irenaeus and Tertullian was the doctrine that prevailed as the orthodox view of the resurrection in the early church. Origen, however, took a somewhat different view as he attempted to interpret the Christian doctrine for the intellectuals of his day.

Origen and an Alternative View of the Resurrection in the Early Church

Origen's doctrine of the resurrection was controversial. He admits in his *Commentary on John* that he is not completely clear on this subject in his own mind. "The mystery of the

---

5. Tertullian, *On the Resurrection of the Flesh* 48–50.
6. Tertullian, *On the Resurrection of the Flesh* 51–56.

resurrection," he says, "is great, and difficult for many of us to understand."[7]

He thinks that the resurrection of Christ "contains the mystery of the resurrection of the whole body of Christ," meaning the church.[8] Like Paul, he speaks of the "newness of life" that follows baptism as resurrection, but also, like Paul, he anticipates a future resurrection.[9] In other words, he does not reduce the New Testament teaching of the resurrection to the new life of the Christian, as some gnostics, at least, did. In an argument closely dependent on Paul's words in 2 Corinthians 4:10, Origen says that Christ "came down to our mortality, that when he died to sin, we, by bearing about in the body the mortification of Jesus, might be able to receive in due order his life forever and ever after our mortality. For those who always bear Jesus's death about in their bodies will also have the life of Jesus manifested in their bodies."[10]

Especially controversial were Origen's speculations about the nature of the resurrected body and its relation to the present physical body. There are two passages where he discusses this subject. One comes from *Against Celsus*, which seems to have been one of the last works Origen wrote, and the other comes from an earlier treatise, *On the Resurrection*, which is lost except for some excerpts quoted by two later church fathers.[11]

The philosopher Celsus attacked the Christian doctrine of the resurrection of the flesh. He seems to have presented it as a raising of the same physical bodies that have died. "Neither we nor the divine scriptures," Origen says in reply, "maintain that those long dead will rise up from the earth and live in the same bodies without undergoing any change for the better." He then

---

7. Origen, *Commentary on John* 10.233; in *Origen: Commentary on the Gospel according to John, Books 1–10*, trans. Ronald E. Heine, FOTC 80 (Washington, DC: The Catholic University of America Press, 1989), 306.

8. Origen, *Commentary on John* 10.229, p. 306.

9. Origen, *Commentary on John* 10.230–32, p. 306.

10. Origen, *Commentary on John* 1.227, p. 79.

11. Origen, *Against Celsus* 5.18–23; the passage from the treatise *On the Resurrection* is preserved only in a quotation in Epiphanius, *Panarion* 64.12.1–17.1.

gives a lengthy interpretation of 1 Corinthians 15 to show the philosopher Celsus that the body that is buried is not identical with the body that is raised, but that the latter is the body that God gives to each. He also discusses 2 Corinthians 5:1–4 in this same context to show that this corruptible, mortal body undergoes a change when it puts on incorruption and immortality. "We do not say," Origen concludes, "that after the body has been corrupted it will return to its original nature, just as the grain of corn that has been corrupted will not return to be a grain of corn. For we hold that, as from the grain of corn an ear rises up, so in the body there lies a certain principle which is not corrupted from which the body is raised in incorruption."[12] In a later passage in the same work, Origen refers to this same "seminal principle" in the soul and argues that the soul, whose "nature is immaterial and invisible," always requires "a body suited to the nature of" its "environment."[13] This means, in practical terms, that when the soul lived in this material world it needed to be clothed in a material or physical body so that it could exist in its environment. Since he assumes that the life following this one will be in an immaterial rather than a material world, the soul will need to be clothed in a body that is not material for that new life.

In the treatise *On the Resurrection*, Origen argues against Christians who think that the bodies that are resurrected will be the same "bodies we have now." He argues instead that even our physical bodies are in a constant state of changing. Each day, for example, food is taken into the body and eliminated from the body. This material substratum of the body, he says, is continually changing, but despite this, the body remains always the same. He attributes this to what he calls the "form" of the body, which persists through all the changes. At the resurrection this form, changed for the better, will enclose the soul once more. Even though the change will be significant, it will still be the

12. Origen, *Against Celsus* 5.23; in *Origen: Contra Celsum*, trans. Henry Chadwick (Cambridge: Cambridge University Press, 1965), 281.
13. Origen, *Against Celsus* 7.32; in *Origen: Contra Celsum*, 420.

same form from this life, just as there is a continuity of identity in a person from infancy to old age. He then uses the argument noted above about the soul needing a body suitable to its place and appeals to the "forms" Jesus, Moses, and Elijah had at the transfiguration. Their forms, he asserts, did not differ from what they had been. He appeals to 1 Corinthians 15 to argue that what is sown is a natural body, but what is raised is a spiritual body. The resurrected body will not be flesh and blood, but it will nevertheless bear the characteristics that characterized the physical body. Origen concludes his discussion of the resurrected body by appealing to Paul's analogy in 1 Corinthians 15 once more to say that "the ear of grain comes to maturity, vastly different from the original seed in size, shape and complexity."[14]

We have looked at three different views of the resurrection taught and believed by Christians in the first three centuries of the church. All of them depend, in some way, on the earliest Christian discussions of the resurrection, which are in the Pauline letters of 1 and 2 Corinthians. The gnostics emphasized the spiritual nature of the resurrection, which Paul discusses, to the complete dismissal of a resurrection of the body. Then we surveyed the view that identified the resurrected body with the flesh of the body in this life, though even here both Irenaeus and Tertullian recognize that the nature of the body of flesh will be altered in significant ways. Finally, we looked at Origen's teaching, which, like the gnostics, dismisses a resurrection of this physical body but nevertheless holds to the resurrection of a body that has a direct link with the body we have known in this life.

The view of Irenaeus and Tertullian was considered orthodox in the later church, and the other two views were both dismissed as heretical. In some respects, nevertheless, Origen's view was not so radically different from that of teachers like Irenaeus and Tertullian, as his later opponents claimed. He tried to show

14. See Epiphanius, *Panarion* 64.12–16; from *The Panarion of Epiphanius of Salamis*, trans. F. Williams (Leiden: Brill, 1994), 145.

how the resurrected body would be both in continuity with, and changed from, this present body. Tertullian, as we noted, attempted the same thing when he distinguished between a substance being destroyed and being changed.

Points for Discussion

1. In your own words, compare and contrast the views of the gnostics, Irenaeus and Tertullian, and Origen on the resurrection of the dead.
2. Read through the two passages cited from Paul in 1 and 2 Corinthians and be able to show what points were used from Paul to develop each particular view of the resurrection.
3. Which of the three interpretations do you think best represents Paul's thought?
4. Which of these three early interpretations of the resurrection do you find most satisfying? Why?

Resources for Further Reading

Irenaeus. *Against Heresies*. In *ANF*, vol. 1. See especially Book 5, chs. 7–9. Also available at http://www.ccel.org/ccel/schaff/anf01.ix.vii.viii.html.

Kelly, J. N. D. *Early Christian Doctrines*. 2nd ed. New York: Harper & Row, 1960. See especially 459–89.

Origen. *Against Celsus*. In *ANF*, vol. 4. See especially Book 5, chs. 18–23. Also available at http://www.ccel.org/ccel/schaff/anf04.vi.ix.v.xviii .html.

Tertullian. *On the Resurrection of the Flesh*. In *ANF*, vol. 3. Also available at http://www.ccel.org/ccel/schaff/anf03.v.viii.i.html.

15

"And They Came to Life and Reigned with Christ a Thousand Years"

The Millennium

> For the Son of man will come in the glory of his Father with his angels, and then he will repay each one as he deserves.
>
> Matthew 16:27

Identifying the Major Personalities

Papias: Bishop of Hierapolis in Asia Minor; died about 130.

Irenaeus: Bishop of Lyons, France, in the last quarter of the second century.

Polycarp: Bishop of Smyrna in the first half of the second century.

Justin Martyr: Christian apologist in Rome in the mid-second century.

Tertullian: Christian teacher in Carthage, North Africa, in the early third century.

Hippolytus: Christian teacher in Rome in the early third century.

Origen: Christian teacher in Alexandria and Caesarea in the third century.

Dionysius: Bishop of Alexandria in the late third century.

Ambrose: Bishop of Milan in the fourth century.

Tyconius: Christian teacher in North Africa in the fifth century.

Augustine: Bishop of Hippo, North Africa, in the fifth century.

This chapter continues the general subject of eschatology, which was introduced in the preceding chapter. There we discussed the resurrection of the dead, a central doctrine in the Christian hope, though we noted considerable disagreement concerning the nature of the resurrected body. This final chapter treats a doctrine that is related to the return of Christ but is relatively marginal to the Christian hope. The return of Christ, accompanied by the judgment and reward or punishment of those judged, is a central Christian doctrine, referred to in several texts throughout the New Testament. The Nicene Creed concludes the long section on the Son of God by saying that he "is coming again with glory to judge the living and the dead."[1] This chapter treats the doctrine related to the return of Christ called millennialism. What view one holds of the millennium has no direct relationship to affirming or denying the return of Christ. The doctrine is included because it is sometimes a point of strife between churches today. It is important to know, therefore, what was thought about the millennium in the classical period of Christian doctrine.

The doctrine called millennialism or millenarianism derives its name from the Latin word that means "one thousand." It is also sometimes referred to as chiliasm, which comes from the Greek word for "one thousand." It teaches that there will be a resurrection of the saints prior to the final judgment and that Christ will return and reign on this earth with the resurrected saints for one thousand years. The details of that thousand-year period are described differently by different authors. All understand it as a time of peace. Some also describe it as a time when the earth will be exceptionally fertile.

1. See the Nicene Creed, quoted in ch. 3 above.

We will look at the source of the millennium doctrine in the Bible and at some passages in both the Bible and some noncanonical late Jewish literature that were used to flesh out the picture of the thousand-year period. Then we will consider the varieties of early Christian millennialism, for there was not complete agreement among those who held the doctrine. Finally, we will consider some in the early church who denied the doctrine of a millennial reign of Christ on earth.

The Biblical and Late Jewish Literature Used to Describe the Millennium

The only place in the Bible where a thousand-year reign of Christ on earth is mentioned is in Revelation 20:4, 6, where the martyrs are said to reign with Christ a thousand years. Revelation 20:5 states explicitly that "the rest of the dead" do not live again until the end of the thousand years. The "rest of the dead," which includes both saints and sinners, are said to be judged in the judgment that follows the final defeat of Satan (Rev. 20:10–13). The whole Christian millennial doctrine rests on how one interprets these few verses in Revelation 20.

Epistle of Barnabas on the Eschaton

He mentions the Sabbath in the beginning of the creation: "And God made the works of his hands in six days, and he made an end on the seventh day and rested on it, and sanctified it [Gen. 2:2–3]." Notice what it says he made an end of in six days, children. It means this: In six thousand years the Lord will make an end of all things, for a day with him means a thousand years. He himself testifies with me, saying, "Behold, a day of the Lord will be as a thousand years [Ps. 90:4]." Therefore, children, in six days—that is, in six thousand years—all things will be brought to an end. "And he rested on the seventh day [Exod. 20:11]." This means, when his Son has come he will abolish the time of the lawless one and will judge the godless and will alter the sun, moon, and stars. Then he will truly rest on the seventh day.

Epistle of Barnabas 15.3–5

Those early Christians who taught a millennial doctrine did so on the basis of their understanding of Revelation 20. They fleshed out the details of their doctrine, however, by taking ideas from several Old Testament texts and other noncanonical Jewish apocalyptic texts. None of the texts used contain any mention of a thousand-year reign of the Messiah. Two Old Testament texts, however, were used later to argue for millennial viewpoints. The first was Psalm 90:4, which refers to a thousand years in God's sight being like yesterday; in other words, a thousand years and a single day are equated in this poetic description of how God's perspective is radically different from that of a human. The other text sometimes used in conjunction with this understanding of a thousand years equaling one day was the story of the seven days of creation in the opening of Genesis. Some early Christians put these two texts together to reckon the duration of the earth and to calculate the time of the end.

Texts from the prophets, especially Isaiah, that speak of peace among the inhabitants of the earth, including the animals, were drawn on to describe the millennial reign, as were texts mentioning the extraordinary fertility of the earth and brilliance of the heavenly bodies, the renewal of Jerusalem, and the appearance of a new temple.[2] This is not an exhaustive list of the Old Testament texts used, but these were key ideas and texts. These Old Testament passages were the raw materials that were worked over and modified in later Jewish apocalyptic literature. The early Christians took up these raw materials from the Old Testament, often as they had been understood in the Jewish apocalyptic literature. We turn our attention now to some of the Jewish apocalyptic descriptions of the end time.

In the latter part of the apocalyptic work known as *1 Enoch* there is a short section referred to as the apocalypse of weeks.[3]

---

2. Isa. 11:6–9; 65:25; Amos 9:13; Isa. 30:26; 52:1–2, 7–10; 54:11–14; 65:17–18; Ezek. 40–48.

3. *1 En.* 91 and 93. In my account I follow the reconstruction in R. H. Charles, *The Apocrypha and Pseudepigrapha of the Old Testament in English*, vol. 2 (1913; repr., Oxford: Clarendon, 1968). The account of weeks 8–10 appears in ch. 91

---

2 Baruch on the Eschaton

And it will happen that when all that which should come to pass in these parts has been accomplished, the Anointed One will begin to be revealed. . . . The earth will also yield fruits ten thousandfold. And on one vine will be a thousand branches, and one branch will produce a thousand clusters, and one cluster will produce a thousand grapes, and one grape will produce a cor of wine. . . . And it will happen at that time that the treasury of manna will come down again from on high, and they will eat of it in those years because these are they who will have arrived at the consummation of time. . . . And it will happen after these things when the time of the appearance of the Anointed One has been fulfilled and he returns with glory, that then all who sleep in hope of him will rise.

2 Baruch 29–30; trans. A. F. J. Klijn, *OTP* 1:630–31

The author divides world history into ten weeks. The first seven are past. They were times of wickedness that reached a climax in the seventh week, described as a period of apostasy. A time of righteousness appears at the beginning of the eighth week. Sinners are delivered into the hands of the righteous. This was probably intended to refer to the messianic kingdom, though *1 Enoch* does not give it this label. The righteous receive houses, and a temple is built for God's glory. The ninth week appears to be an extension of the eighth. True religion is revealed to all humanity, sin is banished from earth, and the world is prepared for judgment. The great judgment occurs in the tenth week. The first heaven passes away and is replaced by a new heaven in which, following Isaiah 30:26, all the lights of heaven are said to be seven times more brilliant. Following the judgment are innumerable weeks that stretch on forever, in which there is no sin.

The author of *2 Enoch* blends the seven days of creation with the words of Psalm 90:4 mentioned above and says that the earth will last for seven thousand years (*2 En.* 32–33). This will be followed by the eighth day, in which time will no longer be reckoned. The author of *2 Baruch*, expanding on Amos 9:13,

---

and that of weeks 1–7 in ch. 93. Charles places weeks 8–10 (ch. 91) immediately after that of week 7 (ch. 93) in his reconstruction.

says that when the Messiah begins to be revealed, the fruit of the earth will multiply ten thousand times. Every grapevine will have a thousand branches, each branch will produce a thousand clusters of grapes, each cluster will contain a thousand grapes, and each individual grape will produce more than a hundred gallons of wine. Manna will also reappear to provide food for those in the end time. After these things, the Messiah will return in glory, the righteous dead will rise, and the souls of the wicked will waste away (2 *Bar.* 29–30). No mention is made of a thousand-year period in this account, though there is a period of blessing for the saints of undefined duration before the final resurrection. In *4 Ezra* the Messiah is said to come and establish a kingdom on earth for four hundred years.[4] No one is resurrected, however, to participate in this kingdom. Only the righteous who are alive when the Messiah comes participate. At the end of this four-hundred-year period the Messiah and all humans die. The world returns to primeval silence for seven days, followed by the dawning of a new age, the general resurrection, and judgment, which rewards some and condemns others to punishment.

These Jewish traditions about a special reign of the Messiah on earth at the end of time, as well as the Old Testament texts noted above, were available to shape the thinking of the author of Revelation 20 as well as the Christians of the second century and later. Christians, however, used these traditions and texts in conjunction with Revelation 20 to fill out the details of the millennial reign mentioned there. We turn now to see how this was done, beginning in the early second century.

Varieties of Early Christian Millennialism

Papias is the earliest witness to millennialism outside Revelation 20. His writings have all perished, so we are dependent on what other early Christians wrote about him. Eusebius says

---

4. *4 Ezra* (also called 2 Esdras) 7.

that Papias claimed to have learned from oral traditions that Christ will rule on this material earth for a millennium after the resurrection of the dead.[5] Irenaeus says that the elders who saw the apostle John, among whom he includes Papias, heard John relate what the Lord taught about the end time when the resurrected righteous dead would reign on earth. The extraordinary fruitfulness of grape arbors is described with the words from 2 Baruch noted above. In addition to grapes, a similar fertility is related of wheat, fruits, seeds, and grass. The animals that feed on this abundant produce will live in harmony, as Isaiah says.[6]

Irenaeus is a witness to these same traditions. He was bishop in France, but he grew up in Asia Minor and had heard Polycarp, a companion of Papias, there. His views show the deep influence of Papias on his own thought. It was Irenaeus who preserved the teachings of Papias about the millennium. He believed that there will be a resurrection of the righteous, who will live in the present world, but the world will have been renewed. He argues that this is just because it was in this world that the righteous suffered. They should, therefore, be rewarded in this world for their suffering. Creation will be restored to its original condition in this period and Jerusalem will be rebuilt like the Jerusalem above.[7] He draws on several of the Old Testament passages we noted in the preceding section to support his millennial thought.

Irenaeus's presentation of the millennium is unique among the earliest Christian writers, so far as we know at least, in that he saw the purpose of the thousand-year period to be to accustom the saints to the glory of God. He refers to it as a disciplining for incorruption.[8] When the thousand-year period comes to an end, the present world will pass away and all humans who have become incorruptible will live with God in the new heaven and earth forever.[9]

---

5. Eusebius, *Ecclesiastical History* 3.39.11–12.
6. Irenaeus, *Against Heresies* 5.33.3–4; see Isa. 11:6–9; 65:25.
7. Irenaeus, *Against Heresies* 5.32.1; 5.35.2.
8. Irenaeus, *Against Heresies* 5.35.1, 2.
9. Irenaeus, *Against Heresies* 5.36.1.

Justin Martyr, writing a little earlier than Irenaeus, recognizes that there are both true and heretical Christians who deny that there will be a millennial reign. But he adds that he, and all Christians who hold correct doctrine, know that there will be a resurrection of the dead, after which they will live for a thousand years on this earth. Jerusalem will be rebuilt and enlarged at that time, as Ezekiel, Isaiah, and other prophets state.[10] Tertullian says that he expects an earthly kingdom of a thousand years after the resurrection. It will be in the Jerusalem that descends from heaven and that Ezekiel and the apostle John have described.[11] Like Irenaeus, Tertullian argues that this reign on earth allows the saints to be rewarded where they have suffered. The saints who participate in this kingdom, however, do not all rise at the same time. They arise earlier or later, as they deserve. The thousand-year reign will be followed by the destruction of the world, and the judgment. The saints then instantaneously become like the angels and are taken to heaven.[12]

Other early Christians understood the millennium in connection with the seven days of creation interpreted as seven thousand years by applying the statement in Psalm 90:4 to the days of creation. The history of the world was divided into seven millennia. The seventh millennium corresponded to the seventh day of creation on which God rested. This was understood to refer to the rest enjoyed by the saints during the thousand-year messianic reign on earth. Those who interpreted the millennium in this way did not draw on the prophetic texts that were so important to the authors we have looked at above. These Christians emphasized instead the idea of rest corresponding to the seventh day of creation or the Sabbath day of history.

The author of the *Epistle of Barnabas* represents this millennial view.[13] Hippolytus also took this approach to the millennium.[14] He

10. Justin, *Dialogue with Trypho the Jew* 80.4.
11. Tertullian, *Against Marcion* 3.24.3–4.
12. Tertullian, *Against Marcion* 3.24.6.
13. *Barn.* 15.3–5; see the sidebar "*Epistle of Barnabas* on the Eschaton," above.
14. Hippolytus, *Commentary on Daniel* 4.23.

says there must be six thousand years of history before the Sabbath of rest comes, the day on which God rested from his labors. The Sabbath day—or one thousand years, on the reckoning of Psalm 90:4—is when the saints will reign with Christ on earth, as John has said in Revelation (or the Apocalypse). Hippolytus reckons time on the basis of the generations from Adam and concludes that Christ first came in the five-thousand-five-hundredth year since the beginning. On this basis Hippolytus considers himself to be living two hundred and fifty years before the millennium. He does not anticipate an imminent return of Christ.

There were varieties of interpretations of the millennium among the early Christians. These interpretations all deviated rather significantly from John's statement in the Apocalypse that spoke only of the martyrs sharing in the thousand-year reign. Those holding these interpretations took the idea of a thousand-year reign of Christ on earth from the Apocalypse and embellished it with ideas drawn from widely scattered texts, most of which had no direct connection with a millennial reign of Christ on earth in their original settings. The gnostic Cerinthus even taught that the millennial period would be one continuous marriage feast in Jerusalem given to lust and pleasure.[15]

The Denial of a Literal Millennial Reign of Christ on Earth

Not all early Christians believed that Revelation 20 spoke of a literal reign of Christ on earth after a resurrection of the dead. Origen was one of those who rejected this view. If we recall his doctrine of the resurrected body from the previous chapter, we can guess that he would have no place for a doctrine that spoke of abundant grapes, wheat, and other things a physical body would use in the life to come. He ridicules those who think the Bible depicts a millennium of sensual indulgence as intellectually lazy and led by their own desires and lusts in their understanding

15. Eusebius, *Ecclesiastical History* 3.28.2–5.

of the Bible. He says these people want their resurrected bodies to have the power of eating and drinking and everything else common to flesh and blood. They think they will marry and have children in the life to come, he says, and that Jerusalem will be rebuilt from precious stones. He says these people believe in Christ but read the Scriptures so incorrectly that they derive nothing beneficial from them.[16]

Origen's disciple Dionysius, bishop of Alexandria, composed two works against an Egyptian bishop named Nepos. Nepos interpreted Revelation literally. Dionysius commends him for his Christian faith and his diligent study of the Scriptures but disagrees strongly with his doctrine of the resurrection and the life to come. He says Nepos's views of the millennium make simple Christians view the kingdom of God in ways that are unworthy, because they think it is going to be like this present life but more given to physical indulgence. Dionysius argues that the book of Revelation cannot be interpreted literally.[17]

In the Latin-speaking West the millennial reign referred to in Revelation 20 was normally taken in a figurative way. Ambrose, bishop of Milan, understood it in relation to the purgatorial system of the church. He took the first resurrection to mean that people who had been righteous would be admitted to blessedness immediately at their death and would not have to suffer purgatory, as the sinners did, before the second resurrection. In North Africa in the fifth century, Tyconius wrote a commentary on Revelation and applied it to the contemporary life of the church. He understands the statement about the saints reigning on earth with Christ to speak of the time between the death and resurrection of Christ and his second coming. The first resurrection, he says, takes place when a person is baptized.[18] Augustine, bishop of Hippo in fifth-century North Africa, never speaks of a literal period of a thousand years or

16. Origen, *On First Principles* 2.11.2.
17. Eusebius, *Ecclesiastical History* 7.24; 7.25.6.
18. Brian E. Daley, *The Hope of the Early Church* (1991; repr., Peabody, MA: Hendrickson, 2003), 130.

Augustine on the Millennium

Some people have assumed . . . that the first resurrection will be a bodily resurrection. They have been particularly excited . . . by the actual number of a
thousand years, taking it as appropriate that there should be a kind of Sabbath
for the saints for all that time, a holy rest, that is, after the labours of the six
thousand years since man's creation, when in retribution for his great sin he
was expelled from paradise into the troubles of this mortal condition. Scripture
says, "With the Lord, one day is like a thousand years and a thousand years like
one day," and, on this assumption, there follows, after the completion of six
thousand years—six of these "days"—a kind of seventh day of Sabbath rest for
the final thousand years, with the saints rising again, obviously to celebrate
this Sabbath.

This notion would be in some degree tolerable if it were believed that in
that Sabbath some delights of a spiritual character were to be available for
the saints because of the presence of the Lord. I also entertained this notion
at one time. But in fact those people assert that those who have risen again
will spend their rest in the most unrestrained material feasts, in which there
will be so much to eat and drink that not only will those supplies keep within
no bounds of moderation but will also exceed the limits even of credibility.

Augustine, *City of God* 20.7; trans. H. Bettenson (New York: Penguin, 1986), 906–7

---

of physical delights for the saints. But he does sometimes speak
of the millennium in a manner resembling those we discussed in
the previous section who interpreted it in conjunction with the
seven days of creation. Augustine sometimes refers to a future
period of rest for the saints on earth. At this time all those who
are in the church falsely will be removed and Christ will rule
over this purified church on earth.[19] He considers the millennium
to be the seventh and final period of history.[20] The purpose of
this period of rest is to focus the faithful on the incorruption of
the eternal eighth day that is to follow the second resurrection.[21]
Later, approximately four years prior to his death, in *The City of*

19. Augustine, Sermon 259.2; Daley, *Hope of the Early Church*, 133.
20. Augustine, *Contra Adimantum* 2.2.
21. Daley, *Hope of the Early Church*, 134.

God, Augustine offers an interpretation of the millennium that resembles that of Tyconius mentioned above. He interprets it to refer to the present life of the church on earth, in which the saints are reigning with Christ. They reign with Christ now, he says, but they will reign differently with Christ in the life to come.[22]

There were faithful Christians in the early church who accepted some form of millennial view based on Revelation 20, and there were others who denied that the chapter indicated anything other than what Christians experience in their present life on this earth. No one ever seems to have been pronounced heretical solely on the basis of his or her understanding of Revelation 20. We should learn from that toleration of diverse views in the early church and let that example guide us in our own thinking about the millennial question.

Points for Discussion

1. How closely do the millennial views of the authors discussed in this chapter adhere to what is said in Revelation 20? Give three examples.
2. Do you think the texts used from the Old Testament and from the late Jewish apocalyptic literature are appropriately applied to Revelation 20? Why or why not?
3. Does the church that you attend hold a particular view of the millennium? If so, which one?
4. Which view of the millennium in the classical period of Christian doctrine appeals most to you? Why?

Resources for Further Reading

Augustine. *City of God*. Translated by H. Bettenson. New York: Penguin, 1986. See especially Book 20. Available online in a different translation at http://www.newadvent.org/fathers/120120.htm.

22. Augustine, *City of God* 20.

Daley, Brian E. *The Hope of the Early Church*. 1991. Reprint, Peabody, MA: Hendrickson, 2003.

Hill, Charles E. *Regnum Caelorum*. 2nd ed. Grand Rapids: Eerdmans, 2001.

Irenaeus. *Against Heresies*. In *ANF*, vol. 1. See especially Book 5. Also available at http://www.ccel.org/fathers.html.

Index